D1550912

The book illumina⸱⸱⸱⸱ ⸱⸱⸱ ⸱⸱ ⸱⸱⸱por-
tant questions: Should compulsory
commitment be a medical or a legal
decision? What are the grounds for involuntary confinement? Is the objective
of commitment to punish, to deter, or to
treat? Are mental health professionals
serving the interests of the patient or
the state? What does the conflict over
civil commitment reveal about broader
issues and ideologies within the mental
health field?

Carefully weighing the rights of the
individual versus the welfare of society,
Managing Madness spells out the in-
adequacies and dangers of involuntary hospitalization, and offers important policy recommendations for both
the courts and the mental health professions.

About the Author

*KENT S. MILLER is Professor of
Psychology and Sociology and Direc-
tor of the Community Mental Health
Research Center at the Institute for Social Research, Florida State University.*

Managing Madness

Managing Madness

The Case Against
Civil Commitment

Kent S. Miller

THE FREE PRESS

A Division of Macmillan Publishing Co., Inc.

NEW YORK

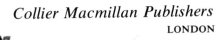

Collier Macmillan Publishers

LONDON

The Free Press
A Division of Macmillan Publishing Co., Inc.
866 Third Avenue, New York, N.Y. 10022

Collier Macmillian Canada, Ltd.

Library of Congress Catalog Card Number: 76-7528

Printed in the United States of America

printing number

1   2   3   4   5   6   7   8   9   10

Library of Congress Cataloging in Publication Data

Miller, Kent S
    Managing madness.

    Bibliography: p.
    Includes index.
    1. Insanity--Jurisprudence--United States. 2. Insan-
ity--Jurisprudence--Great Britain. I. Title.
KF480.M54   346'.73'013   76-7528
ISBN 0-02-921280-4

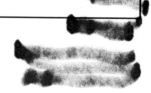

To

B C D M

Some paradox of our natures leads us, when once we have made our fellow men the objects of our enlightened interest, to go on to make them the objects of our pity, then of our wisdom, ultimately of our coercion.

Lionel Trilling
The Liberal Imagination

Contents

Preface   xi

1. Background   1

2. The Experiences of Kenneth Donaldson and Jim Fair   19

3. The Grounds for Hospitalization   36

4. Mental Illness and Dangerousness   57

5. The British Experience   75

6. Involuntary Hospitalization: A Medical or a Legal Procedure?   93

7. Possibilities of Reform   121

Notes and References   143

Bibliography   164

Index   179

Preface

The basic theme of this book is that any state-imposed hospitalization or restriction on personal liberty that is based on an individual's mental state is subject to question. Indeed, the intervention of the state for any therapeutic reason ought, we think, to be a rare event. This is not a radically new position, and a number of the ideas that follow will be familiar to those who have pursued the argument over involuntary hospitalization. But the issue is one of particular importance at this time. We are in a period in which the criminal law has been steadily relinquishing control over individuals, while the domain of the mental health professionals has expanded in a number of directions. As a consequence, a wide range of conditions (including sexual disorders, alcoholism, and drug addiction) are now subject to inspection or treatment by such professionals. There has been increasing confusion as to whether the intent of such treatment has been to treat, to deter, or to punish, and controversy over preventive detention in the name of mental health has steadily mounted.

Things seem to be coming to a head at this particular time. On the one hand there has been a move to recognize the rights of mental patients, and the courts in particular have played a prominent role in bringing about such change. Although admissions to state and county mental hospitals have continued to rise, the average length of stay has markedly decreased and the total number of people resident in the hospitals has dropped considerably. But on the other hand there is noticeable the beginning of a backlash to the deinstitutionalization that has taken place, along with a newly expressed interest in the "rights of the families of mental patients" and a concern about the alleged dangerousness of mental patients turned loose in the community. This climate of opinion will make it difficult to maintain reforms regarding involuntary hospitalization and runs counter to the thrust of recent court decisions.

People like Thomas Szasz have written persuasively and at length on the inappropriateness of involuntary hospitalization and the abuses attendant to it. Much of the argument has been based on case histories, case law, comparative studies, and analysis of the ideology of the professions involved. My purpose here is to carry the argument a step further by examining the results of recent, empirically based research. Whenever social science is used to formulate public policy there is a particular need to tie recommendations to data, and that is the major justification for this book.

The research and clinical work that I have been involved in over the last twenty years, combined with my review of the research of others, leads me to believe that civil commitment for mental illness is wrong. It is wrong in that it is practiced in a highly selective fashion; it frequently involves the violation of individual rights; it is predicated on false premises; it usually does not achieve its avowed purposes; and it is wasteful of resources and damaging to the mental health profession. These are strong statements, but I am convinced that they follow from the available facts.

In this book I have attempted to review the evidence impartially, but by now we all recognize the difficulty of maintaining such a posture, for the same facts may lead different people to very different interpretations and recommendations. One of the major themes of this book is that much of what is done in the name of mental health is ambiguous in nature—ambiguous in that values are involved and in that there is an underlying theme of concern with the social order. Not to recognize the possible biasing effect of my own perspective, as well as the role of values in the "discovery" of facts, would be a serious error. I have tried to be objective. The best corrective to any distortions that have occurred will be the reasoned responses of those who hold another outlook.

Two other points need to be made here. First, in the trade-off between the rights of the individual versus the good of society, I tend to come down on the side of the individual. The policy recommendations which follow are tempered by this bias—one obviously not held by everyone concerned with issues of compulsory hospitalization. The second point is that I do not by any means impugn the conscious motives of the majority of mental health professionals. Instances of deliberate and malicious railroading of people into mental hospitals are probably rare (and once in a mental hospital, it is much easier to get out than it was just a few years ago). The blatant use of hospitalization for political purposes, not uncommon in Russia, is uncommon in the United States. On the other hand, it seems equally clear that some actions taken in the name of mental health and medical treatment are suspect and in need of a radically new understanding.

There can be no doubt about the existence of a large number of people who are disturbed, isolated, depressed, and in need of support. These people deserve attention—but not the kind that we have been giving. It may be that we are entering a new period of reform in our institutions; but reform tends to be limited and short-lived, and professional

organizations and institutions have never been noted for as-
tute self-criticism. Thus there is a need to continue to mar-
shal pertinent evidence and hold it up for public evaluation.

OUTLINE OF THE BOOK

Chapter 1 contains a brief historical description of the
handling of the mentally ill, some information regarding current practice, and a sketch of the causes for controversy.

Chapter 2 consists of two case histories which illustrate
some of the problems involved in civil commitment and
some of the controversial questions that have not yet been
dealt with by the courts. Any number of stories such as
these could have been used to illustrate the problems involved in involuntary hospitalization, but these were chosen
because the writer had first-hand information regarding
them and both are quite recent.

Chapter 3 contains an analysis of the factors which influence or determine which individuals are selected for involuntary hospitalization. This is followed by an evaluation
of the significance of judgments regarding dangerousness
(Chapter 4) and a comparative study of involuntary hospitalization in England, which illustrates the commonality of
issues involved in two rather different systems of mental
hospital care (Chapter 5).

One of the major unresolved issues in compulsory hospitalization has to do with whether such hospitalization
should be a legal or a medical decision. Chapter 6 deals with
this subject and contains policy recommendations which
stem from an analysis of the current role of the court and its
officers.

The final chapter contains a summary of the policy recommendations, their implications for the mental health professions, and some thoughts on parallels with the civil commitment of the mentally retarded and criminal offenders.

Throughout the book I have used terms such as "mental patient," "mental hospital," "mental illness." These are misleading terms, which perpetuate confusion and mask the nature of the problems involved. I use them reluctantly, as a matter of convention and convenience.

I am grateful to former students and colleagues with whom I have researched and argued the issues of civil commitment, in particular to C. Allen Haney, Sara Beck Fein, and Joel See. Their very significant contribution to this book is reflected in the frequency with which their work is cited.

A number of people have made helpful suggestions after reading all or part of the manuscript at various stages: Elane Nuehring, Dale De Wild, John Monahan, Betty Miller, and various graduate students. The book is much improved because of their critical comments.

Appreciation is expressed to Jim Fair for providing access to the records relating to his experiences with the courts and the state mental hospital.

1.

Background

*It is not by confining one's neighbor that one
is convinced of one's own sanity.*

Dostoevski

WE HAVE NEVER had a clear understanding of how to manage the people we consider mad. In earlier times we burned them at the stake, bored holes in their heads to release the "demons" thought to reside therein, placed them on ships to be dropped at the next port, or locked them up with criminals and the poor. More recently we have refined techniques of psychosurgery, applied insulin and electrical shock, and employed a wide range of drugs. Methods of treatment have varied in popularity, but for the last several hundred years there has been one consistent theme to them—that of exclusion and confinement.

The places of confinement employed have been called by different names, but their function has been essentially the same and the recent use of the word "hospital" has not made all that much difference. The people in our mental

1

institutions have primarily been the poor, immigrant and minority groups, the aged, and others with minimum social skills and power—people who in one way or another have offended our sensibilities or have simply been unable to "make it" in the community. We now realize that for the most part we have operated warehouses which have offered little in the way of treatment and much that has encouraged the very conditions and behaviors we set out to correct. Periodic cries for reform have had some effect, but usually a short-lived one.

As a result of some things that we have learned within the last decade or two, it may be that we are now at a point at which substantial change is possible. For one thing, we have learned that we cannot distinguish the mad from the sane with any degree of reliability. This was recently demonstrated in a simple experiment in which a number of eminently sane people had themselves committed to mental hospitals across the country.[1] Although these "patients" behaved in the hospital as they normally did outside, they were not seen by hospital staff as different from others on the wards, all were given a psychiatric diagnosis, and much of their behavior was judged to be pathological. Later, staff members of the hospitals involved were told to be on the lookout for other "normals" who would be sent through the regular admission process. No such normals attempted to enter the hospitals, but the expectation caused admitting officials to identify a number of their regular admissions as the fake patients. This particular study was just one of a long series indicating confusion in our criteria for identifying people needing hospitalization and in determining who is mentally ill.

In addition, recent surveys have shown that the great majority of patients in our hospitals do not need to be there, even when judged by conservative standards.[2] This has been learned not only from surveys but from the experience of releasing a number of patients without harmful consequences. The resident patient population in state mental hospitals has decreased dramatically (from a peak of 559,000 in 1955 to 308,000 in 1971—a decrease of 45 percent), although admission and readmission rates have soared (836,000 people treated in 1971).[3]

Thus, on the one hand, we have learned that admission to a mental hospital can be an arbitrary process and unnecessary in many instances, while on the other hand we are processing a steadily increasing number of people. In the late 1960s there were hopes that with the development of community mental health centers, state hospitals could be closed. (California made specific plans to close its institutions.) But the mental health centers have not provided the anticipated screening and treatment, and the flow to the hospitals has continued.

In spite of changes in our conception of mental illness and treatment techniques, a large proportion of admissions continue to be involuntary, reflecting the continuing belief that confinement is the appropriate response to many troublesome people. But is it? On what grounds does the state involuntarily hospitalize so many of its citizens? What are the objectives of such confinement? Why the high rate of involuntary admissions in the face of repeated attempts to significantly reduce it?

These are important questions, not only because of their significance for the individuals directly involved but because the answers can be instructive in broader matters. The mental health movement in America has been remarkably successful. As with most successes, critics have appeared and the movement is beginning to experience internal conflict.

There is a rapidly developing controversy regarding the basic models of mental illness, the role of the mental health professional, and the nature and function of mental institutions. An intensive focus on what may appear to be a rather narrow issue—involuntary hospitalization for mental illness—can serve as a concrete way of increasing our understanding of some of the broader conflicts and ideologies within the mental health field.

A BRIEF LOOK BACKWARD

An examination of current practice should take place within some historical perspective. I shall mention only a few major events and themes, since excellent, detailed histories have recently been provided by Albert Deutsch, Michael Foucault, and George Rosen.[4] David Rothman has placed the discovery of the asylum in the United States within a social context and drawn a number of inferences for the current scene.[5]

Until medieval times, the mad were left at liberty as long as they presented no special problems. Any unusual attention given to the emotionally or mentally disturbed came from family or friends, with the victim expected to provide compensation whenever possible. By the fifteenth century there were moves to exclude the mad by simple measures such as placing them on ships with instructions to the captain to discharge them at the next port. (It was this relatively common sight of "ships of fools" that led Bosch to create the painting of that title.) The typical response at the next port was to return these troublesome people to their native city, and thus for a period the mad wandered back and forth across Europe.

The sixteenth century saw the development of special

institutions for the insane, culminating, in the seventeenth century, in what Foucault called the great period of confinement—not only for the mentally ill but for a variety of troublesome people. Throughout Europe there were institutions like the Hospital General in Paris, which contained the unemployed, the idle, vagabonds, criminals, and the insane. At one point, one out of every 100 citizens of Paris was confined there, with 10 percent of these estimated as insane.[6]

Initially, the goal of these institutions was containment and the maintenance of social order, but this shifted later on to a concern with providing work for those confined and having them contribute to the general prosperity. By the eighteenth century the causes of poverty were understood to be something other than individual sloth, and thus it was no longer considered appropriate to confine the poor merely because of their poverty. Confinement was to be restricted to the bad and the mad, and early on there were forces pushing for the separation of these two groups. Behind the push for separation was a concern for the criminals, a feeling that it was not fair to subject them to the peculiarities of the mad. This contrasts with our current viewpoint, according to which the negative effects are seen as moving in both directions. Although the trend is to define criminality as the result of sickness or disease, the feeling that a distinction can be made between the criminal and the mentally ill is reflected in current struggles between state departments of corrections and departments of mental health. Neither department wants to deal with individuals judged to belong in the other camp. But with the exception of those judged to be criminally insane, separation was achieved and confinement came to be carried out in specialized institutions. (This separation may currently be in the process of breaking down, as illustrated by the fact that in 1975, in the face of marked overcrowding in its prisons and empty beds in its mental hospitals, Florida transferred a number of prisoners to the hospitals.)

The next significant event in the handling of the mentally ill involved an awareness that all mad people did not have to be physically constrained. The names of Tuke and Pinel are most frequently mentioned in this regard. In 1796, William Tuke, an industrialist, helped the Society of Friends establish a retreat at York, England, which was dedicated to the abolition of physical restraint of the mentally ill. This retreat is usually described as a model of humane treatment, but Foucault suggests that another kind of restraint was imposed: the inmates were given minority status and treated as children. "The keeper intervenes without weapons, without instruments of constraint, with observation and language only." There was a heavy emphasis upon social amenities and religion in addition to work. Foucault concludes that the process produced the "perfect stranger," albeit without physical restraints.[7]

Phillippe Pinel followed Tuke by introducing reforms in Paris. He broke the chains of the mentally ill, but his approach continued to involve repressive measures, such as the shock of cold showers and direct threats to enforce desirable behavior. It should also be noted that Pinel did not abolish all confinement. The dungeon was reserved for the religiously fanatic, those who resisted work, and those who stole. "The three great transgressions against bourgeois society, the three major offenses against its essential values, are not excusable, even by madness."[8]

But whatever errors and imperfections we now see in the efforts of Tuke and Pinel, those efforts offered a lesson of significance: the mad could be handled without physical constraints. Directors of asylums in this country in the

1840s knew this to be true,[9] but we seem to have forgotten it. In the 1970s, we still have locked wards, chemical restraints (drugs) are in wide use, and dangerousness is very much a part of the public stereotype of mental illness.

A second lesson from Tuke's and Pinel's work, also soon forgotten, was that most of the problems of the mentally ill are moral in nature, involving violations of accepted customs or patterns of social or personal relations. And it was within this framework that the medical man became involved with the management of the mentally ill. The doctors' initial powers were of a moral and social nature.

> The doctor's intervention is not made by virtue of a medical skill or power that he possesses in himself and that would be justified by a body of objective knowledge. It is not as a scientist that *homo medicus* has authority in the asylum, but as a wise man.[10]

With the shift to positivism and scientific objectivity it was forgotten that the physician initially received his authority to treat the mentally ill from his status as a moral person, and eventually mental illness came to be understood as a disease "just like any other disease." An elaborate classification system was developed, and there was much interest in diagnosis and some talk about treatment.

The management of the mentally ill in America followed the pattern outlined above for Europe.[11] At first, care was provided by family and friends. Individuals who were believed to be violent or dangerous were handled under police powers.

With the development of the first institution solely for the mentally disabled at Williamsburg in 1773, the problem of developing proper commitment procedures was recognized. Prior to this, commitment was an easy and informal process. Virginia passed its first law providing for involuntary commitment of mental patients in 1806, legislation which gradually evolved during the latter part of the nineteenth century to set the pattern for much of our current law. In particular, in 1845, the Massachusetts Supreme Court ruled that an individual could be restrained only if dangerous to himself or others, and this ruling has served as the foundation for most state statutes today.

A number of mental hospitals were constructed in the late nineteenth and early twentieth centuries; they were characterized by poor staff and a primarily custodial function. The mental hygiene movement led by Clifford Beers had a humanizing effect, but it was short-lived and the hospitals continued to exist essentially as warehouses.

Our more recent history has been characterized by a steady expansion of the mental hospital system. The first decrease in resident patients began in 1956, primarily as a result of the availability of psychotropic drugs. Opinions differ as to whether it was the direct action of the drugs which was significant, or whether the existence of the drugs affected staff attitude and made possible the administrative changes which led to a decrease in residents. In any case, state expenditures for mental hospitals have continued to rise, with maintenance costs alone increasing 54 percent between 1966 and 1971, when the figure was over $2 billion.[12] It seems clear that the hospitals are going to continue to function for some time to come and that the practice of involuntary hospitalization is far from dead.

THE SIGNIFICANCE OF INVOLUNTARY HOSPITALIZATION

Why is the issue of hospitalization of importance in the 1970s? In the first place, many people are involved, with over 800,000 patients being treated annually in state mental hospitals. Of 404,000 admissions in 1972, 169,000 (42 percent) were involuntary civil commitments.[13] The proportion in some states runs as high as 90 percent. Although the current trend is toward a proportionate increase in voluntary admissions, this trend has fluctuated considerably, and as we shall see later, a question can be raised about the distinction between involuntary and voluntary commitments. The distinction is blurred when it is realized that voluntary patients do not have the freedom to leave whenever they choose and the threat of involuntary commitment is always present.

Until recently, involuntary hospitalization frequently included adjudication of the patient as incompetent. Thus, aside from the patient's loss of freedom, there is a loss of a number of civil rights as well. In California, for example, incompetency involves sixteen potential penalties, seven more than those imposed on a convicted felon. Depending upon the state in which a person lives, one may lose the management of one's financial and legal affairs; one's driver's license; the vote; the right to free communication through the mails; the freedom to marry, divorce, or have children; the right to pursue certain vocations—e.g., medicine, cab driving, cosmetology, or the training of guide dogs for the blind—the right to own firearms; and the freedom to purchase intoxicating liquors.[14] Even though the trend is to separate hospitalization proceedings and the determination of incompetency, losses such as the above continue to be common.

Involuntary hospitalization is also of importance because it may serve as the first step toward the development of a lifetime "career" as a mental patient. The process of being publicly identified and labeled as mentally ill, given its effects on self-esteem, can set up a self-fulfilling prophecy which increases the likelihood of the victim's self-definition as mentally ill. It is still debatable whether the effectiveness of treatment outweighs the negative effects of hospitalization, a point to which we will return later. For those who argue that there is now very little stigma attached to having been a mental patient, note should be taken of an ordinance passed in Long Beach, New York, late in 1973, which bans anybody requiring "continuous" psychiatric, medical, or nursing care or medication from being registered in any of the city's housing facilities.[15] This is a rather neat twentieth-century parallel to Bosch's Ship of Fools.

If for no other reason, the hospitalization process is of significance for economic reasons. Involuntary commitment involves time and activity on the part of the courts, additional record keeping and safeguards at the hospital, and, most of all, the basic daily cost of hospitalization.

Finally, the subject deserves attention because so many significant relevant groups are not well informed about it. This includes the public in general, mental health professionals, and legislators. The rights of the mentally ill have moved into the forefront of the legislative agenda. Nearly every session of a state legislature has before it some proposed legislation regarding the handling of people alleged to be mentally ill. Arguments are put forth both to increase legal protections and, on the other hand, to turn the entire process over to physicians. Recently several of our larger states have massively revised their laws relating to hospitalization and have taken widely differing approaches. It is unlikely that all of them have taken the most desirable routes. A number of states are likely to be undergoing massive changes in the near future, and they should have the benefit of whatever facts are available. The problem takes on added significance at this time in light of a current trend to provide for the involuntary hospitalization of alcoholics, drug addicts, and sexual offenders.

The authors of a recent extensive study of hospitalization in seven states concluded that most doctors and lawyers, public officials and welfare agencies, and even mental hospital personnel were not well informed.

> The initiation of public hospitalization is generally viewed as a mysterious process about which little is accurately understood and about which it is difficult to obtain reliable information. Many social welfare agencies to whom inquiry or requests for assistance concerning treatment of the mentally ill might be made are apparently not well informed on the subject. The same is true of most public officials, even of the police, who have wide direct contact with the problem. As far as we can tell, the same is also true of most doctors and lawyers. Moreover, legal counsel is seldom sought by patients and their families when confronting the bafflements of the initiation process. Indeed, the initiation of public hospitalization seems to be characterized by unguided groping in a darkness of ignorance, misinformation, and confusion.[16]

SIGNS OF UNREST

Involuntary hospitalization for mental illness is currently a "hot issue," and all indications are that it will continue to pick up steam. Arguments about this specific issue take place against a broader background of controversy regarding the nature of mental illness and the role of mental hospitals and mental health professionals.

The disease model of mental illness under which we have operated for the last 150 years is under heavy attack, the argument being that the label of mental illness is inappropriately applied to most of the people currently so designated. Rather than a disease in the usual sense, what we are said to be dealing with are problems in living or violations of social, legal and ethical norms. This perspective is consistent with the author's view, but it will not be argued here in any detail. The major criticisms of the disease model may be found in the writings of Thomas Szasz, Irving Goffman, Nicholas Kittrie, Ronald Laing, Thomas Scheff, and Ronald Leifer. Clearly there has been a shift from an exclusive focus on things inside the head of the person to a concern with social systems and external events.

We have already referred to hard questions regarding the effectiveness of treatment, the harmful effects of hospitalization, and the role of the mental health professional. With respect to the latter, there is growing controversy over the extent to which mental health professionals are primarily therapeutic in orientation as opposed to being correctional or control agents. Szasz in particular makes a strong argument that the attitude of the mental health professional is not the one most often voiced—which is that of exclusive concern for the welfare of the client. On the contrary, he sees a basic conflict in that the great majority of such professionals are paid by the state while, at least with respect to state hospitals, the vast majority of the patients are drawn from the powerless and the lower classes.

Mental health agencies are increasingly charged with the responsibility of dealing with irritating, troublesome people in the community—reflecting a conflict that has existed over time but has not been clearly recognized. In fact, Massachusetts is the only state that has overtly acknowledged that nonconformity is equated with mental illness. Until 1971, under the state statutes a person "likely to conduct himself in a manner which clearly violates the established laws, ordinances, conventions or morals of the community" was considered mentally ill.[17] This definition brings into focus the political aspects of hospitalization, aspects which we have tended to keep in the dark.

There are, as well, more specific signs of the degree of ferment in this field:

- Nationally televised programs have dealt exclusively with involuntary hospitalization.
- Discussion of involuntary hospitalization in the professional journals has increased, as reflected in the number of references cited in this book.
- Social scientists and physicians have banded together to form the National Association for the Abolition of Involuntary Mental Hospitalization.
- The American Bar Association has conducted several national surveys on the topic and recently established a commission on the mentally disabled.
- Projects based in law schools have had as their focus the rights of patients and have shown a particular interest in involuntary hospitalization.
- A number of recent court decisions have been concerned with involuntary hospitalization.
- The American Civil Liberties Union has taken on as a special project the rights of the mentally ill.
- A number of "mental patients' rights" groups have been established.
- The American Psychiatric Association has established a

committee to study the political abuses of psychiatry in the United States, and the American Psychological Association has shown a parallel interest.

- The Society for Individual Freedom in England is conducting a national investigation of abuses in psychiatric hospitalization and treatment.
- Several books have recently been published detailing the political uses of psychiatric hospitalization in Russia.
- In the U.S., Congressional hearings have dealt with the political uses of commitment.
- The President's Commission on Mental Retardation has as a major concern the law as it applies to the mentally retarded citizen.

The attack on involuntary hospitalization has come from both the left and the right, and all of this suggests that we are entering a new period of widespread concern. There are people who would argue that there have been dramatic changes within the last few years, and clearly there have been changes. But it can be argued that things have not gone far enough, that abuses continue to be far too common, and that if anything the tide of change is already beginning to ebb in the face of evidence which calls for continued action.

Signs of a backlash have been most obvious in California. Under the administration of Governor Reagan plans were made to close all of the mental hospitals, presumably for the purpose of patient welfare but possibly also as a way of cutting the state budget. As a result of the protests of patients' families and of some 16,000 employees of the mental hospital system who feared for their jobs, these plans were reversed.[18] Complaints were made that not enough consideration was being given to persons close to the mentally ill.

Law enforcement personnel also complained, as illustrated by the statement from a representative of the Santa Clara County Sheriff's Department that "our jail population has at least tripled with the people who require hospitalization or antipsychotic medication. We pick them up for loitering and mischievous mischief."[19] And the newspapers contained frequent references to the dangerous behavior of former mental patients.

New York has also had its problems. The mental health system has been accused of drug misuse, mismanagement of funds, lack of staff attention to patients, abuse of patients, and lack of personalized treatment.[20] Accusations such as these have been leveled against nearly every state system at one time or another. What has been new is the charge that the rapid discharge of insufficiently prepared and chronically institutionalized persons has placed an unnecessary burden upon local communities. Many of these patients have been described as living in slum housing, hotels, rooming houses, or nursing or proprietary homes where they receive no care, and where conditions are worse than in the hospitals which they left.[21]

The problem is that because of the general reaction to the way that deinstitutionalization has been carried out, progress that has been made in curtailing involuntary hospitalization may be lost. Former patients are being described in phrases such as "finding themselves on the other side of locked doors," making it difficult to generate concern for those locked on the inside. And mental patients can be expected to be included in the mounting feeling that in general the courts and legislatures have been too sensitive to the rights of individuals, particularly offenders, and not sufficiently sensitive to the needs of society and of those offended against.

VOLUNTARY AND INVOLUNTARY HOSPITALIZATION

Hospitalization for mental illness differs from the usual procedures employed with general medical problems in that it is regulated in detail by statute. The states have tended to follow the model developed by the National Institute of Mental Health in 1952, *A Draft Act Governing Hospitalization of the Mentally Ill,*[22] modifying it here and there. A detailed review of the statutes, such as that provided by the American Bar Association,[23] makes them appear exceedingly complex. But the major categories of hospitalization are limited to informal, voluntary, emergency, and involuntary; and for practical purposes there are two categories, voluntary and involuntary. Much of the material in this book is based upon this dichotomy, but it should be recognized that in operation even this distinction is blurred and can be misleading. The distinction is supposed to rest upon the individual's acquiescence, with voluntary admission calling for an affirmative application from the individual with an absence of compulsion. Under involuntary proceedings this acquiescence is absent; instead, the decision to hospitalize is usually made by a court, an administrative tribunal, or a specified number of physicians.

Involuntary hospitalization occurs under one of two conditions: to wit, the state exercises its authority to commit either under the *parens patriae* doctrine or through its police power. The state's *parens patriae* authority stems from its obligation to provide protection and treatment for those who cannot provide for their basic personal needs as a result of a mental disorder. In contrast, the state's police power is used to protect the public rather than to further the

interests of the individual. There are a number of refinements to this distinction between the two powers, but it is
this essential difference that needs to be kept in mind.[24]

The distinction between the two powers tends to get
blurred in most state statutes in that the grounds for commitment are usually worded so as to include both a finding of
mental illness and/or of dangerousness to self or others, and
a determination of the need for care or treatment. If definitions are provided they are usually vague and circular: e.g.,
''mental illness is any condition which substantially impairs
an individual's mental health.'' The blurring of the distinction between the *parens patriae* and police powers is even
greater in their application.

What needs to be made clear is that the voluntary patient
is also subject to restraint, usually for up to five days, during
which time the hospital may institute proceedings for involuntary hospitalization. More importantly, as we shall see
later, the existence of the power to hospitalize involuntarily
serves as a threat to encourage voluntary admission. There
are frequent references in the literature to physicians using
this power in exactly this way; the patient is told that he
needs to be in the hospital and is given a choice of entering
under one provision or the other. Confirmation of this was
found in a recent study in Illinois in which a majority of
patients admitted voluntarily were already under some form
of official custody, and voluntary admissions occurred in 35
percent of the cases which came to the court for involuntary
commitment hearings.[25] The voluntary route is preferred by
the hospital in many instances because it involves fewer
procedural safeguards and thus is administratively easier.

A parody of the meaning of the word ''voluntary''
characterizes the situation in Russia, where only about 4
percent of all admissions are classified as involuntary. But a

"voluntary" admission may be one that is initiated by a doctor, a family member, or even a labor union official. The phrase "voluntary admission" is also inappropriately applied there to the commitment of children. Parents have almost total discretion, with the child's power limited to whatever influence he can bring to bear upon the parents and physician.[26]

On the other hand, it should be noted that some patients who are classified as involuntary admissions actually enter willingly and without protest. Indeed, a recent study has shown that some patients deliberately manipulate events so as to gain admission and remain in the hospital.[27] The size of this group is not known, but its existence further confuses questions of legal admission status.

The major issue raised in this book is that of the continued and widespread use of involuntary proceedings, particularly when there seems to be unanimous agreement that the voluntary procedure is more desirable. Voluntary admission is said to encourage early treatment, increase cooperation with the physician, eliminate the potential trauma of court involvement, and avoid many of the due-process questions associated with involuntary hospitalization.

2.

The Experiences of Kenneth Donaldson and Jim Fair

THE TWO CASE HISTORIES which follow illustrate in some detail the major problems and unresolved questions arising from involuntary hospitalization, and they thus provide a useful background for the issues discussed in this book. The Donaldson case was reviewed by the United States Supreme Court in the summer of 1975 and received wide coverage in the press (much of it misinformed). As we shall see, the findings of the Court in the Donaldson case will have major implications for the entire mental health system, but of even greater importance are those questions raised but not answered by the Court.

The story of Jim Fair is less well known but no less important in illustrating issues within the courts and the mental health system which need exploration. Technically the Fair case involves a criminal commitment, in that he faced a charge of trespass and the court raised a question about his competency to stand trial. But in fact, the major motivations and conflicts present are characteristic of civil commitments

and illustrate the not uncommon experience of sending individuals to mental hospitals and subsequently dropping the
charges against them.

THE CASE OF KENNETH DONALDSON

In December, 1956, the father of Kenneth Donaldson initiated commitment proceedings against him because he
was thought to be suffering from "delusions." In January,
1957, a county judge found Donaldson, age 49, to be a
paranoid schizophrenic and committed him to care, maintenance, and treatment at the state hospital in Chattahoochee,
Florida. He was to be committed for what the judge said
would be "a few weeks" to "take some of this new
medicine," but it turned out that he was confined for nearly
fifteen years. For most of the period from 1957 to 1971,
Donaldson was held in close confinement on a crowded,
locked ward with sixty other people, about a third of whom
had criminal charges pending against them.

The details of Donaldson's condition as of 1956 are not
clear. He denied having any serious problems, but there
were suggestions that he felt that there was some kind of
conspiracy organized against him and that on occasion the
food that he was served had a strange odor. In the entire
record there is no indication of any dangerous behavior on
his part of any kind, at any time. Yet he was denied the
privilege of moving freely about the hospital grounds, and
his frequent attempts to gain release through state and federal courts were unsuccessful.

Unlike many of the residents of state mental hospitals,
Donaldson had several people on the outside who were
willing to assume responsibility for him. In 1963, Helping

Hands, Incorporated, a Minneapolis organization which sponsored halfway houses for mental patients, offered to accept him and see that he received treatment from the Minneapolis Clinic of Psychiatry and Neurology. Dr. J. B. O'Connor, Superintendent of the Hospital at Chattahoochee (and Donaldson's former physician), rejected the offer on the grounds that Donaldson could be released only to his parents. This was a totally arbitrary ruling and inappropriate in that Donaldson was 55 years old at the time, and his parents were too infirm to take care of him.

But he had other sources of support. Between 1964 and 1968, John Lembcke, a longtime friend of the Donaldson family, tried on four separate occasions to obtain his release, offering him a place to stay and appropriate supervision and care. The hospital authorities agreed to this under certain conditions—e.g., a notarized statement of agreement from Donaldson's aged parents. But whenever Lembcke met a given set of conditions new ones were required, and he finally despaired and quit trying in 1968. In spite of evidence that Lembcke was a stable, competent, and concerned professional man, Dr. O'Connor said of his last request, "This man must not be well himself to want to get involved with someone like this patient, who even the recent visiting psychologist considered dangerous. Recommend turn it down."

Thus Donaldson remained in Chattahoochee against his will and with little prospect of release. Treatment was nonexistent, since as a Christian Scientist he had rejected electroshock treatments and some medication. He was given "religious" and "recreational" therapy, meaning that he was allowed to attend church and participate in the limited recreational activities available at the hospital. For one eight-to-nine-year period he talked with his psychiatrist

for a total of less than two hours. It is clear that his confinement was simply enforced custodial care.

In 1971, Donaldson attempted to bring a class action suit
requesting appropriate treatment for all patients in the state
mental hospital. This petition was dismissed by the Federal
District Court, and in August, 1971, Donaldson filed an
amended complaint attacking the constitutionality of the
civil commitment statutes. Later this complaint was with-
drawn, and with the aid of the American Civil Liberties
Union and the Mental Health Law Project, suit was
brought against Dr. O'Connor and other physicians on the
staff of the state hospital. It alleged that they had acted in
bad faith and with disregard for his constitutional rights with
respect to: the denial of grounds privileges and occupational
therapy; the refusal of psychiatrists to speak to him; and the
obstruction of his discharge despite a recommendation by a
staff conference that he be given a discharge and the presen-
tation of a signed parental consent. In short, Donaldson
charged that the hospital's superintendent, along with other
staff members, had intentionally and maliciously deprived
him of his constitutional right to liberty.

After a four-day trial in November, 1972, a jury awarded
Donaldson $38,500 in compensatory and punitive damages,
to be assessed against two of the defendants, O'Connor and
Dr. John Gumanis. In April, 1974, this finding and the
award of damages were upheld by the Federal Court of
Appeals, which at the time was the first Court of Appeals
hearing on the issue of the right to treatment under the Fourteenth Amendment.[1] The court held that when the rationale
for confinement is that the patient is in need of treatment,
then the Constitution requires that minimally adequate
treatment be in fact provided. It went on to say that regardless of the grounds for involuntary civil commitment, a per-

son confined against his will at a state mental institution has "a constitutional right to receive such individual treatment as will give him a reasonable opportunity to be cured or to improve his mental condition." It is important to note that the opinion of the court implied that it is constitutionally permissible for a state to confine a mentally ill person against his will in order to treat his illness, regardless of whether his illness renders him dangerous to himself or others.

O'Connor then appealed to the Supreme Court, which handed down a unanimous ruling in June, 1975.[2] The Court elected to deal with the narrow question of every man's constitutional right to liberty and to bypass other issues raised in the lower courts. The opinion of the Court was that the jury had properly concluded that O'Connor had violated Donaldson's constitutional right to liberty:

> In short, a state cannot constitutionally confine without more a nondangerous individual who is capable of surviving safely in freedom by himself or with the help of willing and responsible family members or friends.

The case was then vacated and remanded to the Court of Appeals because that court had not considered whether the trial judge erred in refusing to give an instruction to the jury requested by O'Connor to the effect that the latter had relied on state law as authorization for the continued confinement of Donaldson.

Various news media headlined the Court's ruling as a "right to treatment" decision, which it had been at the Federal Court of Appeals level. But Chief Justice Burger, in a concurring opinion, made it clear that the Supreme Court was not confirming the lower court's ruling that there is a constitutional right to treatment. In his explication of the court ruling, Burger wanted to make it clear that the court was not empowering the state to confine the mentally ill solely for the purpose of providing treatment. In order to justify the deprivation of liberty, additional conditions must exist.

Implications and Unresolved Questions

The experience of Kenneth Donaldson is of interest both because it typifies in some respects the experience of many civilly committed persons and because of the questions not considered by the Supreme Court.

The grounds for the original commitment were, in the words of the Supreme Court, "less than clear." Donaldson claims that he was interviewed through jail bars for less than two minutes by two psychiatrists, and that the commitment "hearing" was conducted in a similar manner. He was not allowed to present witnesses or ask questions. Throughout the entire court record there was no evidence of dangerousness to self or others. Yet he was kept on a locked ward against his will for years—in spite of the fact that the hospital staff felt that he was capable of caring for himself on the outside, something which he had done for years before his confinement and which he continued to do after his release in 1971.

As with most patients in mental hospitals, Donaldson found difficulty in his many attempts to reach a sympathetic ear outside of the hospital. State and federal courts repeatedly denied his petitions, and local bar associations were not responsive. It is not unreasonable to believe that part of the lack of response was because he was writing as a patient within a mental hospital, and thus ipso facto not to be taken seriously.

He was referred to as a patient, but he had in essence no direct contact with a doctor. He was apparently viewed as more of a nuisance than anything else, and for reasons that are not altogether clear, his release was denied even though the opinion of the staff was that he could function successfully on the outside.

There is no question that the Supreme Court's June, 1975, decision will have a considerable impact upon the mental hospital system. If it is enforced, many involuntary patients will have to be transferred to voluntary status, released, or labeled as dangerous. And if the damages against the two physicians are allowed to stand, state hospital psychiatrists are likely to be much more prudent in their decisions regarding involuntary hospitalization. It is also true, Florida mental health authorities claim, that as a result of the Donaldson decision competent psychiatrists may be even less eager than heretofore to work in state institutions.

But possibly of greater importance are other issues raised but not dealt with by the Supreme Court. The Court's only definitive ruling concerned involuntary custodial confinement—specifically, the Court found that "mental illness" alone cannot justify a state's locking up a person against his will and keeping him indefinitely in simple custodial confinement. The Court went on to note that the state cannot confine the mentally ill merely to ensure them a living standard superior to that which they would enjoy on the outside or in order to save its citizens from exposure to nonconforming behavior.

The court did *not* decide:

1. whether mentally ill persons dangerous to themselves or to others have a right to treatment upon compulsory confinement;

2. whether a nondangerous, mentally ill individual may be confined for the purpose of treatment;
3. whether, when, and by what procedures a mentally ill person may be confined by the state;
4. whether an involuntarily committed person has a right to refuse treatment;
5. the standards of proof involved in civil commitment proceedings; or
6. whether different causes for commitment justify different conditions of confinement.

These are important questions which can be expected to come before the Court in the near future. The remainder of this book is designed to enlighten the search for the proper answers.

THE CASE OF JIM FAIR

On March 12, 1973, Jim Fair was transferred from the Hillsborough County Jail in Tampa, Florida, to a state mental hospital in Chattahoochee. Considered a dangerous criminal, he was handcuffed for the six-hour ride in a sheriff's car. The trip was a confirmation of a prediction Fair had made to a reporter three years earlier:

> I've either got to go behind humor to build an audience or I've got to go behind religion. As a humorist they won't lock me up. As a religious man they won't lock me up. But if I keep doing what I'm doing they're going to lock me up.

What he kept on doing, for years, was irritating a lot of people. Defining himself as the champion of the "little people," he turned to the courts for relief on a number of issues. He sued to eliminate large filing fees so that a poor man could run for public office. He tied up a thirty-million-dollar expressway until the legal authority to sell bonds expired. At public hearings he repeatedly fought giant private utilities—particularly the General Telephone Company—when they requested rate increases. He sued for the right of mental patients to have access to an attorney. In Fair v. Fair, he successfully sued himself as Supervisor of Elections in Hillsborough County to obtain the right of non–property owners to vote in school bond elections.

Jim Fair was a general irritant in other respects as well. His name appeared on ballots for congressman, mayor, city clerk, and member of the State Public Service Commission. He picketed, protested, and filed law suits with such abandon that there was some talk of charging him with barristy (use of the courts for harrassment). He expressed a passionate dislike of and distrust for lawyers, and repeatedly argued that they should not be elected to public office.

Fair's nonconformist stance was particularly confusing to a lot of Tampa people since he came from a refined Southern heritage and a family that had produced a number of surgeons, attorneys, and other successful professionals. (He changed his name from Farrior to Fair to reflect a concern for justice and the rights of the little man.) Nor was his behavior consistent with what would otherwise be expected of an Annapolis graduate who had retired as a lieutenant commander after fifteen years of service in the Navy. His appearance—long hair, bright red beard, casual dress—didn't help either.

But he did accomplish things. A *St. Petersburg Times* reporter, Dudley Clendenen, who had known Fair since childhood had this to say:

Because of him, the poor now have freer access to public office—he helped focus public attention on the regulation of the state's giant power and telephone companies long before the average consumer knew how or where to complain about rates and services—I know that countless political questions, large and small, have been better ventilated because Searcy [his middle name] was there to stir a wind.

Things began to go badly in 1970 when Fair was removed from the office of Election Supervisor on the grounds of malfeasance and misfeasance. In January, 1973, he was sentenced to a six-month jail term for assault. He had kicked a woman—who he claimed was picking up a bottle with the intention of hitting him—in the rear. The usual penalty for this offense was a $100 fine and a suspended sentence. While in jail on this charge he was brought back to the court of County Judge A. M. Merckle to answer a charge of trespass after warning. Fair had been on public property—the Tampa Convention Center—seeking petition signers in order to qualify to run for the office of congressman and had failed to move on after warnings by law enforcement authorities. There is some question about the constitutionality of the ordinance and of the use to which it was put in this instance, but that is not particularly pertinent at this point. What is pertinent are the events that followed.

When Fair was brought before the court, Judge Merckle immediately raised the question of whether he was competent to assist counsel in defense against the charge of trespass, and two psychiatrists were appointed to examine him. He refused to talk to one of them, and a simple recommendation was made that he be held for observation. The other psychiatrist, Dr. Robert H. Coffer, talked with Fair and diagnosed him as a paranoid schizophrenic, but not dangerous to himself or others. On the opinion of this psychiatrist (the state law required evaluation by two physicians) Merckle found Fair to be incompetent, and this troublesome man was carried off by the sheriff to the state hospital.

Fair was placed on a locked ward but quickly gained the freedom of the hospital grounds and continued playing out his usual role by filing law suits, organizing voter registration drives, and generally serving as an advocate for other patients. After several months at the hospital the medical staff was unanimous in the opinion that he was competent to stand trial, and two staff psychiatrists were quoted as saying that in their opinion he had never been mentally ill and that he was not a danger to himself or others. The State Hearing Examiner, Jon Caminez, noted that testimony taken at a hearing on May 25, 1973, conclusively revealed that Fair was not suffering from a mental disease within the meaning of the relevant Florida statutes and was not dangerous to himself or others. Caminez went on to say that evidently the man had been sent to the hospital for some other reason and that this was a tactic "used by political systems opposed to democracy." He called for an investigation into the events surrounding the commitment, stating, "I find it incredible that any person could find Mr. Fair incompetent to aid his own counsel in his own defense."

Fair was returned to Tampa to stand trial before Judge Merckle on the trespass charge. On July 11, in spite of the overwhelming and conclusive evidence provided by the hospital staff, another competency hearing was held. Dr. Benjamin Ogburn, Fair's treating physician at the hospital, again testified. In response to questions about the three and one-half months that Fair had been held in the hospital, he explained that extensive study was needed because of the contradictory diagnosis made by Dr. Coffer. Following psychological testing, interviews, and constant monitoring of Fair's behavior the staff found no indications during the entire period that he was incompetent or that he suffered from an illness known as paranoid schizophrenia. They found no mental illness needing treatment and specifically stated that coercive treatment was not indicated. A second psychiatrist, a Dr. Chambers, sat through the twelve-hour hearing in Tampa, which included a two-hour opening statement by Fair, and also concluded that he was competent. The only contradictory evidence was that of Dr. Coffer, who stood by his original diagnosis of paranoid schizophrenia, which was based on a sixty-five-minute interview in which Fair thought he was "sitting down for a conversation with an educated man." Dr. Coffer again admitted that Fair was not dangerous.

For reasons best known only to Judge Merckle, the unanimous opinion of the psychiatrists at the state hospital, based upon study and observation from March 12 to June 22, was not acceptable to him. He must have given equal weight to the testimony of Dr. Coffer, who had enjoyed one interview with Fair some six months earlier. The court asked for two additional psychiatric opinions. Fair refused further examination on the grounds that he had just been under intensive observation for a long period of time and that he did not care to incriminate himself. Merckle's response was to rule that he must return to the state hospital at Chattahoochee.

Throughout the various proceedings, Fair made it clear that he was interested not only in leaving the hospital but also in having the original court determination found to have been in error. Not only had he lost his real estate salesman's license and his driver's license, but a number of his court petitions and suits had been thrown out because of the incompetency determination.

On July 26, Hearing Examiner Jon Caminez assembled the participants once again, and there was a rerun of the testimony of the hospital psychiatrists. One of the doctors was quoted in a newspaper as having said that even if a person such as Fair believed that an action of the government was corrupt, it was not a sign of paranoid schizophrenia. In the aftermath of Watergate, this certainly must stand as one of the great understatements of all time.

At this July 26 meeting, the Hearing Examiner noted that all of the testimony indicated that Fair was not dangerous to himself or to others. In spite of this, Fair testified that shortly after his return to the hospital from Tampa, he had been given a knockout shot, put in a belt and handcuffs, and then placed in isolation for sixteen hours after he and another patient refused to leave the mess hall when ordered to do so by an orderly. He claimed that they had been allowed only ten of the thirty minutes allotted for eating. The hospital superintendent explained that Fair had been put under restraint for a few hours for his own protection. Fair was described as having been loud and upset and having waved his arms, which "in a mental hospital could cause other patients to attack him." In short, it was claimed, the isolation and restraints were applied not because Fair was judged to be dangerous, but for his own protection—a rationale that has been offered over the years for whatever we do to people in our institutions.

At this July hearing, an additional piece of information came out. The woman who accused Fair of kicking her in the buttocks had also been in the mental hospital but was released to stand trial on unrelated charges. Fair was originally charged with assault and battery after an incident in the living room of James Edward, an attorney, where Fair was alleged to have kicked one Lynn Pannell. Pannell and Edwards were the only witnesses, and they succeeded in convincing a six-person jury to convict Fair of assault. Less than a year later, Edwards charged Pannell and a companion with beating him up and robbing him. Later, Edwards charged that Pannell had committed perjury in her testimony against Fair. Still later, Edwards was murdered and Pannell was indicted. At a sanity hearing requested by her attorney, two court-appointed psychiatrists testified that she was a chronic paranoid schizophrenic, and she was ordered to the state hospital at Chattahoochee.

Somewhere in the course of this complicated process Fair was given a chance to have the assault and battery charge quietly buried and forgotten. The *St. Petersburg Times* reported that the Assistant County Solicitor told Fair that the assault and battery charge would be put on the absentee docket if he would pay whatever medical costs Pannell had sustained (one visit to a physician). Fair refused, even though the other side of the offer was that "Judge Merckle will throw the book at you if you don't accept." And he did throw the book at him, in the form of six months in jail and a year's probation—a severe sentence for a simple assault charge.

On August 2, 1973, the Hearing Examiner ordered the release of Jim Fair from the state mental hospital system with the statement that he should not be accepted again unless circumstances drastically changed. The *order* was not immediately effected as Judge Merckle contended that the Hearing Examiner could not disturb the court's original commitment order. The Florida Department of Health and

Rehabilitative Services, which supervises the mental hospitals, was reluctant to release Fair until he could be returned to the court's jurisdiction. A solution seemed to be at hand when Fair requested that he be allowed to enter the Jacksonville Naval Hospital for rest and recuperation. Caminez issued a short order agreeing to this, but it developed that the hospital reported that it had no room for Fair. The situation was finally resolved when Judge Merckle dropped the trespass charge and Fair was permitted to leave the hospital, some six months after the question of his competency had first been raised.

Implications and Unresolved Questions

Considerable attention has been given to abuses in institutional psychiatric practices, but very little has been said about the failure of the courts to be concerned about the rights and welfare of allegedly mentally ill people.[3] In writing the legal opinion and order which led to Fair's release, the Hearing Examiner noted that the following basic Constitutional rights had not been granted Fair:

1. the right to trial by jury;
2. the right to a fair trial;
3. the right to a speedy trial;
4. the right to an attorney; and
5. the right to confront witnesses.

It should also be noted that no time limit was placed upon the period of Fair's detention. Florida Criminal Rule 3.210 states "the order of commitment shall request that the defendant be examined and a written report be furnished the court stating (1) whether there is a substantial probability that the defendant will become mentally competent to stand trial within the foreseeable future and, if so, (2) whether progress toward that goal is being made.'' It is safe to assume that in this instance Judge Merckle either was ignorant of the appropriate law or deliberately disregarded it. A number of other technical points of law were ignored that need not be elaborated here. All of them reinforce the observation that the law was generally disregarded and that Merckle used the mental health system in an arbitrary and inappropriate manner in order to punish a troublesome person. (It should be noted that the doctrine of judicial immunity makes it almost impossible to successfully bring suit for judicial malpractice and damages.) As we shall see in Chapter 7, this is not an unusual record, in that commitment proceedings are rarely legal in any strict sense of the word.

But the hard times of Jim Fair illustrate more than an arbitrary exercise of the power of the court. The reliability of psychiatric diagnosis is brought into question, as there is no reason to suspect the good faith of Dr. Coffer when he made his diagnosis of paranoid schizophrenia, a serious psychosis. Yet after four months of observation the other examining physicians could find no evidence of mental illness. This is not a minor difference of opinion. It makes understandable Fair's refusal to talk with one of the psychiatrists or to submit to further examinations, and raises the interesting question of whether an alleged mentally ill person should have the right to remain silent in order to avoid self-incrimination.

The Jim Fair story also reflects the common association in the public mind between mental illness and dangerousness. Although none of the psychiatrists involved judged Fair to be dangerous, he was transported between court and hospital handcuffed in the back of a sheriff's car, a not unusual practice in delivering patients to mental hospitals.

In one respect Fair was fortunate. The psychiatrists at Chattahoochee did not take the common stance of playing it safe by assuming the presence of disease. Like many of us, Jim Fair had enough quirks so that it would have been possible to build a case against him without too much difficulty. Indeed, Fair must have been under considerable stress from having been labeled a paranoid schizophrenic and, in his view, railroaded into the hospital. The two 300-mile rides with sheriff's deputies from Tampa to Chattahoochee while handcuffed also must have done little for his mental health. Under these circumstances the strongest of people could be expected to show some symptoms of paranoia, but Fair held up well—so well that after considerable study his physicians were clear and consistent in their opinion. Jon Caminez, the Hearing Examiner, was also forceful in his investigation and decisions.

If all of this could happen to Jim Fair, an intelligent, educated, and articulate public figure, it is easy to suspect that there must be many cases of others without these attributes that never come to our attention.

3.

The Grounds for Hospitalization

THE OBJECTIVE OF THIS CHAPTER is to put into perspective the process by which people enter mental hospitals involuntarily. For the most part it has been assumed that the procedures involved are direct and rational: people become mentally ill, their behavior makes them visible and troublesome, and physicians and the courts determine the person's need for institutionalization on the basis of his or her medical condition and potential dangerousness. But this perspective has been severely questioned in recent years on the basis that there are a number of personal, social, and structural characteristics which influence the decision to hospitalize, and that these characteristics are much more important than the psychiatric status or behavior of the individual.

These contrasting viewpoints are frequently referred to as the *medical model* or *psychiatric perspective* and the *societal reaction perspective*. Simply put, according to the psychiatric perspective, people enter mental hospitals because they have a serious psychiatric disorder. Those who hold to a societal reaction or labeling perspective argue that

36

behavior must be understood in terms of the reactions of others and in reference to a particular social and situational context. That is, the decision to label someone as mentally ill and recommend hospitalization implies a set of values and standards by which someone is judged to be deviant, and the process very much involves the persons or groups making the judgment.

These contrasting perspectives, particularly with respect to hospitalization, have been debated extensively by Thomas Scheff and Walter Gove.[1] This chapter does not speak to all of the issues which Scheff and Gove have raised, but by reviewing some additional evidence it will hopefully carry the debate a little further. We expect that the reader will find the evidence convincing that in many instances hospitalization is a highly selective and arbitrary event, regardless of arguments about the psychiatric condition of the persons involved.

Basic questions have been posed by the results of field studies of the mental health of the general population over the last fifteen to twenty years. Detailed reviews reveal a surprisingly high prevalence of psychiatric disorders in the general population, with as much as 80 percent of the population found to have mild to incapacitating symptoms.[2] One of the most widely quoted studies, the Midtown Manhattan survey, found that approximately 25 percent of residents studied had severe psychiatric symptoms and only approximately 20 percent were symptom-free.[3] Recent investigations have consistently reflected high rates of mental illness, and the more intensive the study and the more direct the contact with the people being studied, the higher the rates. No one claims that these studies yield reliable and valid measures of mental illness, as there are many definitional and measurement problems involved, and many of the studies are not comparable. But when we compare these figures with the proportion of people who are recognized and labeled as mentally ill, it is apparent that only a small fraction of people judged to have serious psychiatric problems get into the mental health treatment system. Scheff, extrapolating from some of these data, suggests that only about one in fourteen is so recognized.[4] An examination of other studies might lead to projections which would be slightly higher or lower than this, but for our purposes a more precise estimate is not necessary. The major point is that people who are involuntarily hospitalized represent only a small proportion of those who might be judged in need of hospitalization. Thus it becomes important to understand the basis of selection. Is selection a rational and objective process? Who is it that gets committed? On what grounds is civil commitment continued?

Before moving on to examine specific studies relating to hospitalization a word needs to be said about the reliability and validity of psychiatric judgments. This is an important issue, because the civil commitment process calls for judgments to be made about the presence of mental illness and dangerousness, the need for hospitalization, and the effectiveness of treatment. The ability to predict dangerousness will be discussed in some detail in the next chapter, while the material to be discussed here has implications for the other questions.

The professional literature contains a number of reviews on the reliability and validity of diagnostic judgments, and they consistently call into question the scientific basis for this aspect of psychiatric practice. (Such skepticism is reflected in the title of one such recent review: ''Psychiatry and the Presumption of Expertise: Flipping Coins in the Courtroom.''[5]) Still another review is not needed here, but the problem of inaccuracy and ambiguity in diagnosis needs to be recognized and serves to explain some of the arbitrary decisions that are made.

VARIABILITY IN INVOLUNTARY HOSPITALIZATION RATES

It is reasonable to expect some variations across time and place in the proportion of the population judged to be in need of hospitalization. Such variation could be based upon differential community attitudes, the availability of alternative services, changing conceptions of mental illness, the number of hospital beds in a given area, and a host of other factors. But even allowing for the operation of these factors, the degree of variation that exists is cause for concern. For example, in 1970, Utah had only one mental hospital patient for every 2,366 persons residing in the state, while the District of Columbia had one patient for every 223 persons living there, a differential of over 1,000 percent.[6] Such variations in rates occur in the absence of significant variations in commitment statutes or in the incidence or prevalence rates of severe mental illness. Furthermore, as Birnbaum has pointed out, there appears to be almost unanimous sentiment that neither first-admission rates nor resident inmate rates for state institutions can be used as valid measures of the incidence or prevalence of mental illness in the general population.[7]

The above comments apply to hospital utilization generally, not to the more specific issues of concern to us, that of variability in the use of involuntary hospitalization. The discussion that follows will focus on this topic and deal with interstate and intrastate variation within the United States, where hospital systems could be expected to be reasonably comparable with respect to factors influencing admission status.

Interstate Variation

Statistics on the admission status of patients nationwide have not been readily available, and although variability across states has been recognized for some time, the range of variation has not been known. For this reason, in 1972 we surveyed State Departments of Mental Health, asking for information for 1970.[8] Wide variability by state was reflected in the proportion of admissions in 1970 that were involuntary—10 percent for Alaska as compared with 96 percent for Florida. Even though these states are poles apart climatically, there is no obvious reason for such disparity in the proportion of individuals needing involuntary hospitalization.

When only the more populous states (those with over 10,000 hospital admissions annually) were examined, the range of involuntary admissions was from 34 percent to 77 percent. Even though for the country as a whole the percentage of involuntary admissions decreased from 1960 to 1970, more than half of all admissions continued to be compulsory in 1970 (53 percent). Several of the smaller states (Delaware, Utah, Wyoming) showed an increase in the proportion of involuntary patients from 1960 to 1970.

Intrastate Variation

Variation in rates of involuntary hospitalization is demonstrated even more strikingly when comparisons were

tion and admission status.[12] These data are subject to more than one interpretation, but there seems to be no question that the associations are real.

There is a consensus regarding the kinds of people who are admitted to our state mental hospitals—to wit, primarily the poor and the powerless. The argument has been made that persons with limited social and economic resources, and thus less social power, have the highest probability of being involuntarily committed. It has been hypothesized that power is positively associated in the United States with being male, white, married, middle-aged, and of relatively high occupational level. If this is a valid hypothesis, we would expect these characteristics to be positively associated with a court finding of competence and subsequent release rather than hospitalization. Again we turn to the Florida studies for evidence on this point.

Haney and Michielutte report a monotonic relation between age and outcome—the older the person the greater the chance that he will be declared incompetent,[13] a finding that has been replicated in two additional studies on Florida populations.[14] At the older age ranges the probability of being declared competent rapidly begins to approach zero.

Table 1 illustrates the significance of age, sex, and race for outcome. If the determination of incompetency is related to a relative lack of power and status, we would predict what See found—that the elderly black female would be the person with the highest incompetency rate. And being an unemployed black is very strongly related to a determination of incompetency.[15] Haney and Fein came to essentially the same conclusions, and similar findings have been reported in at least one other study.[16]

As would be expected, there are some variations and in-

TABLE 1. **Number and Percentage of Cases Found Competent by Ethnicity, Age, and Sex**

	SEX							
	Males				Females			
	White		Black		White		Black	
AGE	NUM-BER	PER-CENT-AGE	NUM-BER	PER-CENT-AGE	NUM-BER	PER-CENT-AGE	NUM-BER	PER-CENT-AGE
1–17	43	27.9	14	35.7	33	39.4	9	33.3
18–24	133	28.6	46	17.4	80	25.0	24	33.3
25–34	148	29.1	70	21.4	123	27.6	45	15.6
35–44	188	31.4	71	32.4	173	24.9	41	17.1
45–64	219	34.7	55	30.9	231	25.1	51	21.6
65–74	66	16.7	14	28.6	64	7.8	12	8.3
75+	71	11.3	10	0.0	82	3.7	15	0.0
*Total**	874	28.3	288	25.0	793	22.7	197	18.8

* The total does not equal the sum of the categories because data on age and sex were unavailable for a small number of cases.

From J. J. See, "Ethnicity and Mental Incompetency Proceedings," unpublished Ph. D. dissertation, Florida State University, 1970. Used by permission.

teractions within the data which do not reflect a simple linear relationship. For example, petitions against black males within the 18-to-24 age group are especially likely to result in a declaration of incompetency. But for the most part, the findings are consistent with expectations.

Haney and Fein report that males escape incompetency findings twice as often as females. See's data confirm the sex difference but not at quite as high a ratio.

On the basis of our knowledge of hospital admissions we would expect marital status to be related to outcome. The following data on this subject are taken from See (p. 136):

Marital Status	Percentage Declared Competent
Separated and Divorced	26
Married	24
Single	15
Widowed	11

The single and widowed are particularly likely to be declared incompetent. The high percentage for the separated and divorced is the only surprise; following our general guide of predicting outcome on the basis of status and power we would have expected this group to be ranked second. But once again, for the most part, the results are consistent with our expectations.

See also found that occupation and outcome were related, with the unemployed, the disabled, and the retired having the lowest competency rate. As expected, there were relatively few people found incompetent at the upper end of the occupational scale, but these professionals and proprietors did not do as well as expected in avoiding hospitalization.

IMPLICATIONS

Taken together, these results suggest that personal characteristics are predictive of outcome in incompetency proceedings. The argument can be made that the distribution of mental illness follows the pattern of personal characteristics reported here—that mental illness is highest among females, blacks, the aged, the single and divorced, and the lowest occupational ranks—and that the results reported here are what would be expected if the psychiatrists and the courts are performing accurately and reliably. But as noted above, there is no clear evidence that mental illness is distributed along these lines, and the hypothesis that social power is related to the outcome of incompetency proceedings remains viable.

THE ROLE OF OTHERS

If the decision to hospitalize is based in a relatively objective manner upon behavior and psychiatric status, then the personal characteristics of the person requesting the hospitalization should be of no significance, nor should it matter which particular path is followed or which agencies are contacted in the process of considering the need for hospitalization. But novelists have been indicating for some time that it does in fact matter, and now there is some suggestive evidence to support their views. Haney, Miller, and Michielutte studied the interaction of social characteristics of the alleged incompetent and of the person signing the petition requesting a hearing, as these characteristics were related to the eventual court judgment.[17] The design involved comparisons based on matched individuals, half of whom had been adjudicated competent, half incompetent. It turned out that knowledge of the age, sex, marital status, education, and occupation of the person requesting the sanity hearing improved the prediction of the outcome of the proceedings. In particular, persons with relatively greater social power (as measured by these personal characteristics) petitioning against a person with relatively less social power had a better than chance probability of succeeding.

The outcome of incompetency proceedings is also related to other contingencies along the path to court action. It makes a difference who first imputes mental illness, who first decides that court action is desirable, and how many and what kinds of people are involved in the process.[18] If the first person to impute mental illness is a mental health professional, there is a high probability of a finding of incompetency. In addition, contact with social and health agencies increases the likelihood of an adjudication of incompetency. Both findings are consistent with what would be expected within the conventional medical interpretation of mental illness. Not too much should be made of these findings, as the amount of variance they explain is relatively small, but they do illustrate the probability of the court's being influenced to a significant degree by factors other than the pathology of the individual.

THE ROLE OF THE COURT

Thus far it has been suggested that the evidence points to decisions about competency and hospitalization as being highly problematic. There is extreme variability from state to state and from county to county, and the outcome is influenced both by social characteristics of the alleged incompetent and by characteristics of others involved in the process. We now turn to an examination of aspects of court procedure as they relate to outcome.

To my knowledge there is only one study which has looked at variability in hospitalization decisions across judges within a given jurisdiction, and it reveals that it makes a difference which judge one happens to come before.[19]

It can be seen from Table 2 that the chance of a white person's being adjudicated competent in Dade County is twice as good if the decision is made by Judge C rather than Judge A. For blacks, the odds of being found competent are

TABLE 2. **Number and Percentage of Cases Found Competent by Ethnicity and Presiding Judge for Dade and Duval Counties, Florida**

| | ETHNICITY | | | |
| | White | | Black | |
JUDGE	NUM-BER	PER-CENTAGE	NUM-BER	PER-CENTAGE
	DADE COUNTY			
A	340	11.5	87	4.6
B	237	18.6	61	14.8
C	151	23.2	43	20.9
	DUVAL COUNTY			
D	125	52.0	49	49.0
E	150	54.0	63	38.1

From J. J. See, "Ethnicity and Mental Incompetency Proceedings," unpublished Ph. D. dissertation, Florida State University, 1970. Used by permission.

four times better in Judge C's court. In Duval County it makes little difference which judge you draw unless you are black, in which case you would do much better to come before Judge D. The idea of "hanging judges," of differences in the severity of sentences given, is not new, and thus it is not too much of a surprise to find variability in the area of civil commitment as well. It should be noted that the figures reported here, as with much of the material in this chapter, do not include any controls for the clinical status of the individual. But the numbers involve a year's activity and are relatively large, and there is no reason to expect a differential distribution of cases to the courts.

Some of the interjudge differences could relate to the particular physicians serving the courts. (In a number of states a physician of any specialty is allowed to serve on an examining committee.) Since the judge rarely disagrees with the recommendation of the examining committee, the composition of this committee is of considerable importance. Again, from the studies in Florida, it was found that one's chance of being declared competent is dependent in part on the medical specialties of the two physicians composing the examining committee. Table 3 contains results which are consistent with expectations.[20] If individuals are trained to detect a particular form of pathology, we would expect them to "find" more pathology than persons not so trained. Thus the odds of being declared competent are markedly better if the committee consists of physicians without training in psychiatry. Table 3 contains one reversal of expectations. Committees containing one psychiatrist, when compared with committees with two psychiatrists would be expected to find a larger percentage competent. The slightly lower percentage of cases judged competent associated with one psychiatrist on the committee may be due to the general tendency of medical people to defer to the opinion of a person with specialist training. Even if allowances are made for the operation of a selective process whereby the psychiatrists see only the most severely disturbed people, there are striking differences in outcome which could not reasonably be attributed to the clinical state of the person. It should be noted that one other study in the Florida series failed to confirm the relationship between medical specialty and outcome, but this was based upon an evaluation which involved a total of only six psychiatrists.[21]

Not only is medical specialty of significance in determining outcome, but it makes a difference how long the physi-

TABLE 3. **Judgments of Incompetency by Committee Composition**

COMMITTEE COMPOSITION	FOUND COMPETENT		FOUND TEMPORARILY INCOMPETENT		FOUND INCOMPETENT		TOTAL
	Number	*Percentage*	*Number*	*Percentage*	*Number*	*Percentage*	
Both Psychiatrist	28	22.6	19	15.3	77	62.1	124
One Psychiatrist	27	16.5	43	26.2	94	57.3	164
All Others	114	40.3	3	1.1	166	58.6	283
Total	169	29.6	65	11.4	337	59.0	571

From C. A. Haney and R. Michielutte, "Selective Factors Operating in the Adjudication of Incompetency," *Journal of Health and Social Behavior*, 1968, 3–239. Used by permission.

cians have been practicing. Fein and Miller report a positive correlation between the collective experience of the committee and its decision. Those examined by a highly experienced committee were much more likely to be declared competent than those examined by a committee of low experience.[22] This is consistent with an earlier finding that decision makers with more clinical experience tend to recommend hospitalization less frequently than their less experienced colleagues.[23]

Other factors related to court procedure—such as the presence of an attorney and the legality of the committee—will be discussed in some detail in Chapter 7.

IMPLICATIONS

These data pointing to the significance of characteristics of the examining committee as they relate to recommendations for hospitalization, combined with interjudge variability in decisions regarding competency, further support the argument that compulsory hospitalization as currently practiced is not based solely on the clinical condition of the individual. Yet surely one's chance of being involuntarily committed should not be dependent on the specialty or experience of the physician who examines him, or on the particular judge who hears the petition.

THE BEHAVIOR OF THE ALLEGED INCOMPETENT

Since a major reason for involuntary hospitalization is the presence of dangerous or troublesome behavior, it is reasonable to expect a difference in adjudication according to differences in behavior. This topic will be discussed in considerable detail below, but within the Florida studies there have been two attempts to obtain data on this point. Haney and Miller interviewed family members who had signed a petition requesting a sanity hearing and asked them a series of questions relating to the behavior of the person petitioned against—including sources of concern, behaviors which caused the most distress, and behaviors which indicated illness.[24] Comparisons were made of the distribution of these behaviors within a group declared competent and a matched group declared incompetent. The only differences in the reported behavior of the two groups was that those declared incompetent tended to have a greater percentage of physiologically based symptoms (19 percent as compared with 4 percent). Surprisingly, the initial troublesome behavior and that which caused the most concern were not differentially associated with outcome.

Questions were also asked regarding critical behaviors (defined as the "last straw") which contributed to the decision that the situation was no longer tolerable. It was assumed that there would be more such incidents in the group declared incompetent, since such incidents tend to be highly visible, have an element of crisis in them, and focus attention on the deviant. Yet, contrary to expectations, such incidents were more frequent among those adjudicated competent. Incidents involving violence or aggression were not markedly different in the two groups (49 percent among those declared incompetent as compared with 42 percent among those judged competent). Behaviors identified as critical and which were potentially dangerous or threatening were not differentially associated with the two groups (44 percent of the incompetent group compared with 48 percent of the competent group).

The second Florida study focused on the association of violent behavior with incompetency proceedings in a single, highly urban county.[25] Violence was considered to be present in a case if the alleged incompetent actually attempted to harm someone else or attempted to end his own life. (This definition probably led to an overestimation of actual violence, since it included minor harm to others such as face slapping as well as suicidal gestures.) Decisions about the presence of violence were based on the incompetency clerk's notes, the affidavit stating the reason for confining the person prior to examination, and the examining physician's reports. Working with this broad definition, evidence of violence was found in 25 percent of the cases. The important question was: Did it make a difference in outcome? The figures in Table 4 suggest that it did not; the presence or absence of violent behavior had little to do with the final decision. They again confirm the notion that the actual behavior of the person has only a limited impact upon involuntary hospitalization.

TABLE 4. **Outcome of Incompetency Proceedings by Presence or Absence of Violence**

OUTCOME	VIOLENCE PRESENT		VIOLENCE NOT PRESENT	
	Number	*Per-centage*	*Number*	*Per-centage*
Competent	35	16.2	104	14.5
Certified*	75	34.7	255	35.5
Temporarily Incompetent	36	16.7	91	12.6
Incompetent	70	32.4	269	37.4
Total	216	100	719	100

* A form of involuntary hospitalization

From J. J. See, "Ethnicity and Mental Incompetency Proceedings," unpublished Ph.D. dissertation, Florida State University, 1970. Used by permission.

This same study also provided some information on the need for detention of alleged incompetents. In Florida, as in most states, when a petition has been filed against an individual the court has the option of issuing a detention order until the time of examination. Such an order is usually issued when the person is considered dangerous to himself or others, and the place of detention is most frequently a hospital or jail. It is a reasonable assumption that people placed under a detention order would have a higher proportion adjudicated incompetent than a group for which detention was not considered necessary. But the data in Table 5, based on eleven Florida counties, run counter to what would be expected on the basis of a rational model of mental illness. Those people judged in need of detention were most likely to be adjudicated competent.

In a separate study, Fein and Miller[26] examined detention and outcome for a one-year period in a single county. They started with three categories: not confined, confined in a

TABLE 5. **Detention Status and Outcome of Incompetency Proceedings**

| | DETAINED | | NOT DETAINED | |
OUTCOME	Number	Per-centage	Number	Per-centage
Competent	165	36.1	230	30.7
Temporarily				
Incompetent	10	2.2	8	1.0
Incompetent	282	61.7	512	68.3
Total	457	100	750	100

From J. J. See, "Ethnicity and Mental Incompetency Proceedings," unpublished Ph.D. dissertation, Florida State University, 1970. Used by permission.

general hospital, and confined in jail; but, in all the contingency percentage tables, the first two categories were very similar for all cross-tabulations. In view of this result and the likelihood that either of these conditions would be less disturbing than confinement in jail, the variable was dichotomized by combining the first two categories. It was expected that confinement in jail would be associated with a higher frequency of judgments of incompetency, since it is reasonable to assume that people so confined would have exhibited more signs of violence or dangerousness. Of the total population studied, 44 percent were confined in jail. Since an earlier analysis revealed that race, sex, and age were correlated with adjudication and place of confinement, first-order partial-correlation coefficients were computed. These were not substantially different from the zero-order correlation of .36. Those held in jail were more likely to be adjudicated competent. Either a selection process operates prior to the examination, or for some reason physicians are more likely to perceive a person in jail as competent. One possibility is that a number of alcoholics are held in jail but stabilize by examination time. Whatever the explanation, this particular study suggests that the use of jail for confinement is unnecessary in many instances.

SUMMARY COMMENTS

We can now return to the questions asked at the beginning of this chapter: How rational is the process of selecting people for involuntary hospitalization and on what basis is the selection made? The research which has been cited has drawn heavily upon a series of studies in Florida, but most of the findings have support from independent studies with different populations. The results are consistent in indicating that the selection process is arbitrary and based on factors which should be irrelevant or of minor significance.

The first thing noted was extreme variability between states and counties. If one political unit commits at a rate which is only a fraction of that of an adjoining unit, with no obvious consequences for patient or community, then clearly the commitment process must be open to question. Secondly, we noted the significance of personal characteristics as they relate to decision making about hospitalization. Age, sex, race, and marital status were shown to have important influences on outcome, with those with low social resources or status more likely to be committed. There is also the not surprising evidence that it makes a difference who it is that wants to hospitalize someone, and how his social power compares with that of the alleged incompetent. The outcome of commitment proceedings has also been related to the composition and experience of the examining committee and to the particular judge involved.

Most importantly, there is evidence that the behavior of the individual is not crucial to adjudication of incompetency. And as we shall see in the next chapter, the major reason for civil commitment, dangerousness to self or others, appears not to be systematically associated with involuntary hospitalization.

In closing this chapter, we should note that the major criticism of the kind of studies that have been reviewed is that they have examined variables without controlling for the psychiatric condition of the patient, and that in fact the actual distribution of mental illnes may follow the patterns suggested. This seems to be a particularly specious argument in view of the overwhelming evidence of the unreliability of psychiatric diagnosis, and the demonstrated role of personal values in psychiatric classification.

4.

Mental Illness and Dangerousness

> *The only purpose for which power can be*
> *rightfully exercised over any member of the*
> *community, against his will, is to prevent*
> *harm to others. His own good, either*
> *physical or moral, is not sufficient*
> *warrant. . . .*

> John Stuart Mill
> *On Liberty*

OVER THE YEARS, potential dangerousness has been a consistent part of our picture of the insane (consider "raving maniac"). This connection in the public mind between mental illness and dangerousness was recently reaffirmed by a survey of county judges and sheriffs in Florida.[1] Seventy-one percent of the county judges who responded and 14 percent of the sheriffs disagreed with the statement that "most of the patients in Florida's state mental hospitals would not be dangerous to themselves or others if they were at liberty," and 95 percent of both groups were opposed to a

57

majority of the patients in such hospitals being retained on a voluntary basis. In light of the fact that these are people who have face-to-face contact with individuals enroute to state mental hospitals—they observe them in the courts and deliver them to the hospitals—these are surprising responses. If the association of mental illness with dangerousness is so strong for these people, then it must surely continue to be strong in the public at large. Certainly it is a major theme in the arguments of those who would retain or even strengthen civil commitment procedures.

Those who argue for stronger commitment laws are prone to cite case histories in which a person's civil rights were protected but he ended up a murderer or a suicide. Indeed, this has happened. But the important questions relate to which acts are sufficiently harmful to society to justify confinement, how frequently such acts are committed by those labeled mentally ill, how good we are at predicting their occurrence, and whether they can be prevented by civil commitment.

Before turning to a review of the evidence which speaks to these questions, a definitional problem needs to be dealt with. State statutes have been notoriously vague in their references to dangerousness, in large part leaving the determination of dangerousness to the whims of the court and of others involved in applying the concept.* In recent years there has been a tendency to extend the definition of danger to include social as well as physical harm. For example, until it was revoked in 1971, a Massachusetts statute interpreted "serious harm" to include behavior which could lead to the loss of a professional license.[2] Even more absurd was

* Dangerousness to self involves different philosophical issues from dangerousness toward others or toward property, and will be discussed in a separate section.

the authorization of commitment on the grounds that the statutory test of "dangerousness to others" had been met when it was feared that the accused would issue checks drawn on insufficient funds.[3] Interpretations such as these involve the casting of a net so large that much of human behavior could be judged as "seriously harmful," and so the term fails to serve as a guide in decision making. Fortunately, several recent court decisions have held for narrower definitions,[4] and during the oral arguments in a recent case before the Supreme Court several justices raised questions about the states' right to involuntarily commit anyone unless they are dangerous.

The majority of researches on dangerousness and mental illness have involved follow-up studies of populations of ex-patients, comparing their behavior with that of the general population. A smaller number of studies have examined circumstances surrounding petitions for sanity hearings or judgments made by admitting physicians at mental hospitals. In addition, there have been a few attempts to correlate levels of general incarceration with incidence of aggressive behavior and with statements of subjective impressions by experienced psychiatrists.

DANGEROUSNESS AMONG HOSPITALIZED AND FORMERLY HOSPITALIZED PATIENTS

Most of the early research on ex-patients pointed to less aggressive behavior among this group than in the general population. Brill and Malzberg examined the arrest rates of over 10,000 former patients in New York and reported a rate of 122 arrests per 100,000 as contrasted with 491 per 100,000 in the general population.[5]

Brennan looked at indirect measures of aggressive behavior among veterans in Massachusetts.[6] After World War II, in order to assist veterans with a service-connected disability in finding work, the state established a special fund to pay claims of aggressive behavior against fellow workers. The act covered some 98,000 veterans, (a number of whom had psychiatric disabilities), but after it had been on the books for eighteen years, only one or two cases had come up under the act, reflecting a dramatic overestimation of the likely incidence of aggressive acts in this population. Brennan's other estimate involved a review of the work performance of over 2,500 former mental patients under standard conditions in industry and Veterans Administration settings. The study covered 75,000 man-days of work, with the finding that lost-time accidents were rare and there was a total absence of injuries due to aggressive behavior.

Additional evidence consistent with that cited above came from a study of 969 criminally insane patients in New York. A court decision (Baxstrom v. Herold) resulted in their transfer from a hospital for the criminally insane to a civil mental hospital—a move which led to much concern and anxiety. There have been at least eight published follow-up reports on the Baxstrom patients, the results of which are summarized by Monahan:

> All concur in the finding that the level of violence experienced in the civil mental hospitals was much less than had been feared, that the civil hospitals adapted well to the massive transfer of patients, and that the Baxstrom patients were being treated the same as the civil patients. The precautions that the civil hospitals had undertaken in anticipation of the supposedly dangerous patients—the setting up of secure wards and

provision of judo training to the staff—were largely for naught (Rappeport, 1973). Only twenty percent of the Baxstrom patients were assaultive to persons in the civil hospital or community at any time during a four-year follow-up of their transfer. Further, only three percent of Baxstrom patients were sufficiently danger-ous to be returned to a hospital for the criminally in-sane during four years after the decision (Steadman and Halfon, 1971). Steadman and Keveles (1972) followed 121 Baxstrom patients who had been released into the community (i.e., discharged from both the criminal and civil mental hospitals). During an average of two and one-half years of freedom, only nine of the 121 patients (eight percent) were convicted of a crime, and only one of those convictions was for a violent act.[7]

Note that these findings are for a group of criminally insane people who would be expected to have a much higher rate of violence than civilly committed patients.

The results of studies mentioned above, as well as several earlier ones, led Rappeport and Lassen to look at pre- and post-hospital arrest rates in Maryland psychiatric popula-tions.[8] The arrest categories examined were murder, man-slaughter, rape, robbery, and aggravated assault. Compari-sons with rates among the general population revealed a higher incidence of robbery among male patients and a higher rate of aggravated assault arrests among females. There were no differences in the other offense categories, and there were no significant differences in pre- and post-hospitalization arrest rates. This was the first study to suggest that arrest rates were not consistently lower among the ex-patient population than among the general population.

Giovannoni and Gurel also raised questions about the early literature suggesting lower rates of disruptive behavior among mental patients.[9] They followed 1,142 veterans with a diagnosis of psychosis, collecting data on the incidence of various types of criminal activity four years after their release from the hospital. One hundred and fifty-six patients were involved in 192 incidents. In comparison with the general population the ex-patients had higher rates of crimes against persons (homicide and aggravated assault). Giovannoni and Gurel concluded that these data supported the view that ex-patient arrest rates were not necessarily lower and for some offenses might be higher. Relatively higher rates of dangerous behavior have also been reported among former hospital patients in North Carolina.[10]

One additional study, focusing on a follow-up of seventy-three patients who had had sanity hearings, deserves mention here.[11] One year after discharge, none of the patients had committed a single serious crime, but there had been incidents of minor assault and automobile accidents. An important conclusion was that those released after sanity hearings had the same quality of adjustment as the hospitalized group.

The findings from these studies comparing formerly hospitalized patients with the general population have not been uniform in their conclusions, but most of the evidence would indicate that dangerousness is not a major problem. Even if future studies should reflect a higher rate of dangerousness among former patients, this group is still certainly not the most dangerous group abroad—consider criminal offenders, drunken drivers.

Studies of patients *within* hospitals have been more consistent in indicating that only a minority are dangerous, even by liberal definitions. The finding of a California legislative committee that less than 10 percent of psychiatric hospital patients were assaultive or violent is typical.[12] This report also noted that thousands of persons were being routinely detained for observation in violation of the law, which authorized detention only for allegedly dangerous persons. In a separate study, similar conclusions were drawn after observation of 116 judicial hearings in California.[13] In 86 of these there was a failure to establish that the patients were mentally ill according to the criteria stated by the judges in interviews; yet the examiners failed to recommend the release of a single one of the patients. From what is known of the California system, which is relatively progressive, there is reason to believe that this situation must be as bad or worse in most other states.

In another western state, the examination of the records of fifty persons who had been involuntarily committed to a public mental hospital revealed that in only five cases did the petitioner allege that the patient was a danger to himself or others. The remaining forty-five were viewed as "irritable," "troublesome," or "difficult to get along with"; yet in all fifty cases the examining physician certified that the individual was a danger to himself or others.[14]

Miller, working with a liberal definition of dangerous behavior among civilly committed patients in a Florida hospital, found that only 18 percent exhibited some form of dangerous behavior at the time of admission, and yet 98 percent of the admissions were involuntary.[15]

Psychiatrists have repeatedly observed that most mental patients are harmless, and the great majority would probably agree with the following position statement by the Council of the American Psychiatric Association:

On the basis of long experience, psychiatrists estimate that about 90 percent of all mental hospital patients are harmless and in no way threaten the community in which they reside.[16]

An even more conservative figure was given at United
States Senate Hearings in 1961, when it was estimated that
for every dangerous mental patient there were one thousand
perfectly harmless patients in institutions.[17]

One other study is worthy of mention here. Macdonald
reported that of 100 patients who were hospitalized for
threatening to kill, three patients actually carried out threats
in the ensuing five-year period.[18] The argument could be
made that hospitalization in these cases was helpful, in that
97 percent did not act on their threats. On the other hand,
the data could be interpreted to reflect the difficulties involved in accurately identifying potentially homicidal persons (since 97 patients did not carry out the threat). Macdonald goes on to present the reasons for not hospitalizing:

Involuntary commitment often provides only brief
protection for society. It may further undermine the
patient's self-respect as well as cause resentment toward the relatives who participated in the court commitment and toward the psychiatrist who was unwilling
to treat him in a local hospital or clinic. Because fear of
recommitment to the state hospital may discourage the
patient from seeking psychiatric help when the next
crisis occurs, the risk of homicide may be increased.

After reviewing the evidence on hospitalization and
dangerousness, Birnbaum concluded:

Available statistics indicate no relationship among
varying suicide rates, rates of psychiatric institutional-

ization, levels of care and treatment in these psychiatric institutions, or any accepted incidence and prevalence rates of severe mental illness. It may well be, therefore, that social factors are a primary determinant in the overall rates of suicide. Thus variations in the rates of psychiatric institutionalization, variations in the levels of care and treatment in public mental institutions, and variations in rates of murder, nonnegligent manslaughter, and suicide do not appear to be related. This is significant in that many laymen frequently seem to erroneously view the institutionalized mentally ill as almost universally homicidal or suicidal. The figures do not support this position. Whether the mentally ill are allowed to remain in the community or whether they are institutionalized would seem to have no significant effect on the overall rate of violent crime or suicide.[19]

We can now return to two of the questions raised earlier: Which acts are harmful enough to call for commitment, and how often do such acts occur? With regard to the first question, clearly we have been vague and overbroad in identifying the behaviors that call for confinement. The answer to the second question is that dangerous behavior among hospitalized patients and ex-patients is relatively rare and markedly less frequent than that of other known groups that are not confined. We now turn to the third question posed at the beginning of this discussion: How well can we predict violence?

PREDICTING VIOLENCE

For the most part, mental health professionals and the courts have assumed that violent behavior can be predicted with a reasonable amount of accuracy. Otherwise state statutes would not include predictions of future violence as a criterion for involuntary hospitalization, and 5 to 10 percent of the 600,000 persons in the United States annually accused of homicide, aggravated assault, rape, and robbery would not be given a mental examination to advise the court of their potential for future dangerous behavior. Yet all of the available facts indicate that the prediction of violence is an extremely difficult task and one which we do very poorly. The empirical studies of attempts to predict violence have been reviewed in detail[20] and need only be summarized here.

The compelling conclusion to emerge from these studies is that violence is greatly *over*predicted. For every person accurately predicted to be violent, there is at least one and possibly as many as a hundred erroneous predictions. This is true whether simple behavioral indicators are used or sophisticated multivariate analyses employed, and whether psychological tests are administered or thorough psychiatric examinations performed. It is also noteworthy that the population used in each of the research studies reviewed here was highly selective and biased toward positive results—consisting primarily of convicted offenders, "sexual psychopaths," and adjudicated delinquents. If it is so difficult to predict violence within groups which have a history of violent behavior, the task is surely next to impossible when applied to individuals who have not committed a violent act.

Considerable attention has been given to the role of psychological tests in predicting dangerous behavior, and there is a wide range of opinion as to their value. For a detailed review the reader is referred to a recent article by Megargee,[21] whose conclusions deserve more attention than they have received. The MMPI (Minnesota Multiphasic Personality Inventory) is generally accepted as the most valid and reliable of the structured psychological tests; it has been the subject of thousands of studies and scoring refinements. The best that Megargee can say about it is that even though it is not accurate for individuals, it can be used to separate groups of people among whom there is a greater likelihood of violence, such as psychopaths or paranoid schizophrenics, from a normal population. His final statement makes it clear that the tests are of little value in predicting violence.

Thus far no structured or projective test scale has been derived which, when used alone, will predict violence in the individual case in a satisfactory manner. Indeed, none has been developed which will adequately *post*dict, let alone *pre*dict, violent behavior. However, our review of the literature suggests that it might be possible to demonstrate that violence could be predicted using psychological tests if programs of research were undertaken that were more sophisticated than the studies done to date.

Even given the possibility of more predictive efficiency, a major problem will remain so far as preventive detention is concerned. Assume, for example, that a test identifies all the murderers in a sample of people while misclassifying only a few. The national homicide rate is six murderers per 100,000. If the false positive rate (identifying people as murderers who are not) is only 1 percent, then for every six murderers correctly identified we would erroneously label as homicidal 1,000 other individuals.

A major difficulty is that even if we improve our prediction rate on the basis of our understanding of personality structure or emotional controls, we would also have to make predictions about the probability of future instigations to aggression. A given predisposition to dangerous behavior may not be provoked in one environment whereas it would be in another. And this is only one reason for the overprediction of violence; a number of additional reasons have been suggested.[22] The person predicting violence seldom has a chance to verify his prediction; the consequences for the predictor are generally much more unpleasant if he underpredicts; and a diagnosis of "dangerous" may function simply as a means to get someone to treatment. Furthermore, prediction of any event which is relatively rare (like dangerous behavior) is difficult; and those who are predicted to be dangerous usually have limited social power and thus are unable to effectively contest the prediction.

Even when we acknowledge the difficulty of accurately predicting violence, the tendency is to recommend carrying on as usual. Note the words of Mechanic, a senior observer of this issue:

> Courts and community agencies must muddle through these difficulties and deal with such problems in the best way they can. The fact that we have difficulty defining and predicting dangerous behavior does not mean that members of the community can disregard such patterns of behavior. And the fact that psychiatrists do not agree on the nature and scope of mental illness does not imply that the law can be oblivious to such matters.[23]

This has indeed been the popular stance. But we are on dangerous ground when deprivation of liberty occurs under such conditions. We are on even more dangerous ground when psychiatrists ignore the statutory requirement that involuntary patients must be dangerous as well as mentally ill and simply commit anyone they feel needs treatment—which is apparently a not uncommon event.[24]

SELF-DESTRUCTIVENESS

Western society has readily tolerated potentially self-destructive behavior in a variety of forms—driving after drinking, daredevil acts of various kinds, etc. But there has been a strong feeling in our society against taking one's life, and in a number of states suicide and attempted suicide are illegal. In recent years there may have been an increase in the number of people who argue that the state has no right to interfere with potential suicides, but for the most part this position has had limited currency. The major justification for intervention has been that a mentally ill person cannot meaningfully be said to have chosen to die—that his suicide would be a product of his illness and that under other conditions the person would elect to live. It is within this framework that most civil commitment on the grounds of danger to self takes place. There are a number of philosophical questions underlying this perspective, but the important question for our immediate purposes is whether involuntary hospitalization succeeds in preventing suicide, merely postpones it, or, possibly, facilitates it.

In spite of the heightened professional interest in suicide over the past ten years, attempts to predict and control it continue to be not much more successful than attempts to predict violent behavior directed towards others. We have learned a few basics—such as the fact that attempted suicides and successful suicides are two different populations, in that most attempters do not unequivocally want to die.[25] But beyond that we are in trouble.

The last decade brought forth suicide prevention centers

across the country and greatly expanded mental health services. The National Center of Suicidology was established; journals were initiated; educational efforts were mounted; research funds multiplied. But the national suicide rate has remained unchanged for the last fifteen years. In and of itself this does not provide a crucial test of the effectiveness of suicide control efforts, but to conclude that they have been effective would entail the unlikely assumption that there has been a dramatic increase in the number of people trying to kill themselves.

Rough estimates indicate that for every successful suicide there are ten attempts. Thus each year in the United States some quarter of a million people attempt suicide, a sizable population. Some of these people are hospitalized, along with a group which is depressed or has threatened suicide.

What happens after hospitalization? Does it make a difference?

It will perhaps not come as a surprise to learn that people who have been hospitalized because of a suicide attempt have a much higher mortality rate than the general population.

Retterstöl has provided a review of about a dozen follow-up studies in European countries.[26] The time of follow-up after hospitalization varied from two to eighteen years, and the studies varied widely in their success in locating the original population. But there were some consistencies. With increased observation time the proportion of suicides increased, as one would expect. The range of subsequent suicides was from 2 to 12 percent, with a mean for all the studies reported of around 4 to 6 percent. An important observation was that repetitions of a suicide attempt were most likely to occur during the first year after hospital discharge. This is consistent with a report by Pokorny, who studied veterans who killed themselves after hospitalization.[27] One-half of his population committed suicide within thirty days of discharge, and five were in the hospital at the time of the act. Shneidman and Farberow report that almost half of the suicides in their studies killed themselves within ninety days after hospital discharge.[28] And a California study revealed that the suicide rate among patients on leave of absence was ten times greater than that of the normal population.[29] These studies, along with a number of others, suggest at the very least that in many instances involuntary hospitalization only delays suicide, and that in some instances it may precipitate it.[30]

There seems to be good evidence that those who attempt suicide and those who succeed come from two different (but overlapping) populations. Those who succeed have been described as moving away from people—in contrast to the attempters, who have been seen as moving toward people. The suicidal gesture is seen as a cry for help, a plea for concern, an act desperately seeking meaningfulness. If this is an apt characterization, the response of involuntarily detaining such a person in a mental hospital seems peculiarly inappropriate. Certainly the cry should not be ignored. Concern and support ought to be expressed. But an argument can be made that commitment and the traditional suicide safeguards may say to the patient exactly what he least needs to hear—viz., that he is incompetent, unpredictable, and no longer responsible for his behavior. In short, that his life is meaningless. There is little direct evidence to support this interpretation, but it seems as plausible as the belief that current practice prevents suicide. Besides, there is good reason to believe that most people who are dangerous to themselves and judged to be in need of hospitalization will enter voluntarily.[31]

A word needs to be said about those who are dangerous to themselves but not suicidal. This group would include those who are sufficiently confused as to wander in the streets, those who fail to eat properly, and those who risk bodily harm in a variety of ways. The argument is made that one must provide for involuntary hospitalization to cover this group. There may be instances in which this would be necessary, but they would probably be rare, and it is possible that most such people would enter the hospital without protest.

IMPLICATIONS AND RECOMMENDATIONS

Despite our desire to think otherwise, there is overwhelming evidence to the effect that violence cannot be predicted with accuracy. The practice has been to markedly over-predict. In addition, the courts and mental health professionals involved have systematically ignored statutory requirements relating to dangerousness and mental illness. These conclusions must be held in mind when attempting to frame policy relating to involuntary commitment under the police powers of the state.

In order to meet the constitutional requirements of due process in balancing the interests of the state against the loss of liberty and rights of the individual, a prediction of dangerous behavior must have a high level of probability, (a condition which currently does not exist), and the harm to be prevented should be considerable. Thus, potential social danger and danger to property should not be permissible grounds for commitment. Although only four states have specifically excluded property from their statutory definition of dangerousness, such a provision would reflect our higher respect for life and the balancing demand that the potential harm must be considerable.

Any policy permitting involuntary commitment under police powers should clearly express the assumption that the function of the court is that of fact finding for the purpose of a judicial determination of the need for confinement. This is a public policy question and not primarily a question for mental health professionals.

If confinement takes place, there should be a short-term mandatory review. Presumably the people committed under this provision would have rejected the option of voluntarily seeking help, and it would be understood that their confinement was primarily for the benefit of the state, not themselves. The number of people being processed under this provision would be quite small and thus not burdensome to the court and to others involved.

All of this leads to the following guidelines: *The basis for police power commitment should be physical violence or potential physical violence which is imminent, constituting a "clear and present" danger, and based on testimony related to actual conduct. Any such commitment should be subject to mandatory review within two weeks.*

Even this attempt to restrict the interpretation of dangerousness to likelihood of physical violence is subject to questions of acceptable due process because of the difficulties in prediction. We have certainly been more tolerant of other groups about whom predictions of dangerousness can be made with greater accuracy—such as drunken drivers. But given the presence of the safeguards recommended elsewhere in this book, abuses should be minimal.

When we consider the use of involuntary commitment to prevent suicide, we find that most of the problems mentioned above apply. Our predictions are equally fallible, and it is possible that intervention may facilitate rather than prevent the action. The situation is further complicated by the civil libertarian argument that a person has an unqualified right to commit suicide. Those who hold to this view would oppose state intervention even if the ability to predict were to become quite high and if effective preventive practices could be developed.

But there is evidence that most suicide attempters do not unequivocally want to die. This fact, coupled with some evidence that short-term detention causes some attempters to change their minds, justifies at least minimal interference. A statute covering commitment for this purpose would need to specify that there must be a high probability of acts which are likely to result in immediate death or serious physical injury. All of the safeguards of full due process would need to be operative, and restraint would have to be limited to short periods. The guiding policy should be along the lines of the following:

Commitment on the grounds of danger to self should be permissible only when there is a high probability of immediate death or serious injury as determined by a reasonable-doubt standard. Restraint should be time-limited, with a maximum of five to seven days.

These provisions should tide the person through a suicidal crisis and, according to the best available evidence, would maximize the saving of lives while somewhat limiting the abuses involved in restraining someone who would not have committed suicide. It is expected that the number of people falling under these provisions would also be very small.

5.

The British Experience

FOR THE PAST TWENTY YEARS there has been a steady
stream of mental health professionals crossing the Atlantic
to study the English mental hospital system. Britain has
been looked to for leadership because of its history of
humanitarian concern for those locked up in institutions,
most recently manifested in the development of the open
hospital and the therapeutic community. More specifically
related to the focus of this book is the British objective of
making less than 5 percent of all hospital admissions compulsory. Since 1959 they have strived to make entrance to a
mental hospital identical with entrance to a general medical
hospital. The widely quoted figure of 90 to 95 percent informal admissions is in striking contrast to the experience in the
United States and raises a number of questions. Are the
figures valid? If so, how are they achieved? What are the
similarities and differences with respect to the hospital systems in the two countries? If the British have eliminated
coercion in hospital admissions except for a very few, why
has the United States lagged so far behind?

BACKGROUND

An early landmark in the English history of the management of the insane was the work of the Tukes in establishing a retreat at York. Although Michael Foucault, in his detailed history, reveals that the retreat was not a liberating environment but rather one based on the instillation of fear, at least one lesson could have been learned from that experience.[1] That was that as early as the eighteenth century it had been demonstrated that the mad could be managed without the use of physical restraint. Between 1839 and 1864 there were a number of hospitals which abolished all modes of restraint, even for patients considered violent.[2] Much of their success was attributed to the small size of the institutions involved (between 125 and 150 patients), but John Conolly showed that restraint could be eliminated without problems in the largest asylum in England. Hanwell had over 1,000 inmates, but within a seven-week period the institution was able to move from the frequent use of coercion to total non-restraint.[3] Yet, even with the aid of our current array of drugs, most contemporary psychiatrists do not believe this possible today.

In England, just as in the United States, there have been periodic expressions of concern over involuntary hospitalization. As early as 1763, a select committee of the House of Commons concluded that sane people were often committed to asylums, and legal moves to increase the proportion of voluntary admissions occurred in 1860, 1890, 1918, 1930, and 1959.[4] Over forty years ago there was strong sentiment in the House of Lords to do away with detention and with any legal intervention in the hospitalization process.[5] These sentiments have resulted in a relatively high proportion of voluntary admissions in England, but there has always been considerable variability by region. In 1931, 45 percent of all admissions in one area were voluntary, while in another area with over four million people, not a single voluntary patient had been admitted by the summer of 1932. Anxiety over admitting patients voluntarily centered around concerns that they would become an elite group within the hospital, that they would consume much time but not stay to be cured, and that the economic depression would result in a number of malingerers seeking hospitalization.

By 1938, 35 percent of total admissions in England were voluntary, and in fifteen hospitals, more than half of all admissions were voluntary.[6] By 1955, 82 percent of all mental hospital admissions in the country were voluntary, and in several hospitals the figure was as high as 90 percent. The latter figure, or a higher one, has been incorrectly cited as a national Figure in numerous studies.[7]

The British have been particularly successful in seeing that regardless of admission status the residents of hospitals are not retained on a compulsory basis, with a recent figure indicating that less than 6 percent are so held.[8] Mapperley Hospital, Nottingham, steadily reduced their number of patients held under legal compulsion so that by 1956 there were none.[9] At the time this was achieved, they had over 1,000 patients and only a fourth had been admitted voluntarily.[10]

It was with an awareness of this history that a Royal Commission on Mental Illness and Mental Deficiency was established in 1954. The work of this commission led to the Mental Health Act of 1959, which constituted a massive revision of the laws relating to mental health. We turn now to an analysis of the major features of this act as they relate to admission status in mental hospitals.

THE MENTAL HEALTH ACT OF 1959

The basic spirit and intention behind the Mental Health Act was to make admission and release procedures from mental hospitals as similar as possible to those obtaining in general medical hospitals. ''Asylum doctors'' were to be brought back into the general body of medical opinion and influence, and the analogy of psychiatric illness to physical illness was to be made as complete as possible, with legal intervention minimized in every way possible. The main principles of the act were described by the Minister of Health as follows:

1. that as much treatment as possible, both in hospital and outside, should be given on a voluntary and informal basis;
2. that proper provision should be made for the residual category of cases in which compulsion was necessary in the interest either of the patient or of society; and
3. that the emphasis in mental cases should be shifted as far as possible from institutional care to care within the community.

It was assumed, then, that a residual category of people existed who would need compulsory treatment, and that psychiatrists could be trusted to make the appropriate decisions. Judicial authority was abolished and a review tribunal was established to provide an appeal procedure for persons after hospitalization had occurred. The basis for compulsory hospitalization was established as similar to that obtaining

in most states in the United States and was equally as
vague: viz., evidence of a mental disorder and/or the need
for institutionalization for the individual's health or safety
or for the protection of others. In most instances where
compulsion was necessary it was hoped that the applicant
would be a family member, although provision was made
for other possibilities.

We should note here a distinction between voluntary and
informal admission, an issue upon which the Royal Commission took a definite stand. The physically ill are not required to make formal application for admission to a hospital (as are voluntary mental patients), but enter on their own
consent, or that of relatives, upon a physician's advice. The
law made it explicit that the mentally ill should be able to do
the same, and thus the 1959 act contains no provision for
voluntary status. This was a deliberate and significant rejec-
tion of the argument that the hospital staff needed notice of
intention to leave so that arrangements for further detention
could be made if deemed necessary, and also of the argument that a signed voluntary admission would mean that the
patient agreed to abide by hospital rules. The only rules
were to be medical, and the patient was to have the choice
of recognizing these or leaving, as he does in a general hospital. In the event, however, that an informal patient could
not be convinced to stay, provision was made to quickly
change his status on the certificate of one general prac-
titioner and one psychiatrist from the hospital.

Analysis of the Act; Section 29

In the discussion which follows, we are interested, consistent with the focus of this book, only in those sections of the

act which relate to involuntary hospitalization of the mentally ill; we will not be concerned with instances involving mental retardation or criminal proceedings.

The four sections of the act of primary interest are Sections 25, 26, 29, and 135–36.

Section 25, "Admission for Observation," sets forth what was intended to be the most common method of compulsory admission, usually involving an application by the nearest relative and the signature of two physicians. It provides for detention for up to twenty-eight days for observation. Section 26, "Admission for Treatment," provides for compulsory admission for up to one year, renewable for another year by a hospital medical officer. Admission is on the signature of two examining physicians. Section 29, "Emergency Admission for Observation," provides for detention for three days on the recommendation of one doctor, in cases of urgent necessity in which the procedure outlined in Section 25 would take too long. Application may be made by a mental welfare officer or any relative. (The implication is that the approval of two physicians, as provided for in Section 25, provides additional protection for the individual. Although there is no evidence that such clauses protect against abuses, lawmakers tend to find them reassuring.) Finally, Sections 135–36, "Police Removal," which are infrequently used, allow the police to remove those who appear to be suffering from mental disorder and to be in need of care and control to a psychiatric hospital (or other "place of safety"), where they may be detained for up to three days.

The use of Section 29 has been a source of considerable controversy and the subject of a number of investigations.[11] The framers of the Mental Health Act had expected admission under this section to be a rare event; yet this section accounts for approximately 10 percent of all admissions and a majority of compulsory admissions. It warrants close examination.

The most striking impression gained from the statistics relating to this section is that of marked variation by region and hospital. Admissions under Section 29 range between hospitals from 3 to 26 percent of total admissions.[12] It is also worth noting that the variation is sensitive to administrative directives. In 1966, the figures were judged to be alarmingly high and the Chief Medical Officer of the Ministry of Health sent out a letter to the superintendents of the mental illness hospitals, calling this to their attention. This resulted, as might be expected, in an immediate decrease, followed by a rapid rise in 1968 and 1969.[13]

V. F. Jones became concerned with the use of Section 29 in the Liverpool region and studied it in some detail over a period of years.[14] He reported a downward trend in the use of Section 29 in this region in the face of a nationally rising rate. After careful study, he concluded that

> most if not the whole of the credit for the marked character of decreases in the Regional figures should be assigned to reappraisals and adjustments of practice by individuals, rather than to development of facilities.

Enoch and Barker, in a separate study, confirmed the impression that the patient's clinical state was not the only consideration involved in the use of the compulsory powers. Hospital policy and individual practice were clearly significant.[15] And Barton and Haider reported that in a sample studied by them, almost 50 percent of admissions under Section 29 were unjustified. They reported the following conclusions in a study of annual admissions in a large hospital in 1964:

1. Sixty-two out of 182 received no letter as to why they were sent in under Section 29.
2. Many said that they would have come informally and stayed on for treatment.
3. In the case of 110 patients, evaluation upon admission did not reveal adequate reasons for the use of Section 29.
4. Observations of behavior on the ward did not justify use of the section.

They proceed to a disturbing observation:

> We estimate that around 5,000 people each year are being compulsorily admitted to psychiatric hospitals without adequate screening of the "troublesomeness" and proper prescription of their true needs to be at home or in a hospital.[16]

The frequent misuse of Section 29 to resolve social problems has been mentioned. Barton cites the example of a teenage girl admitted to care under Section 29 not because of madness, but simply as a result of a quarrel with her father. He remarks that admission under this section is usually not urgent, that the condition has usually been present for some time, and that the purpose of the admission is frequently to remedy a difficult social problem.[17]

There is still another point to be considered. If the provision were necessary, it would seem that a fair proportion of people admitted under it would need to stay involuntarily for treatment. That is, if the situation constituted enough of a crisis to require involuntary hospitalization, it seems unlikely that it would be resolved within seventy-two hours. Yet within three days of admission a very substantial proportion of patients are changed to informal status.[18] Considerable doubt about the soundness of the involuntary process has also been occasioned on the basis of the behavior of the people involved. Studies have shown a surprisingly low number of attempted suicides, and some patients are said to present no psychiatric abnormalities whatever on admission. In one year-long study, no differences in aggressive behavior were noted between formally and informally admitted patients.[19] In fact, a follow-up study of the St. Francis Hospital observation ward in London revealed that in one sample, the incidence of aggressive behavior was higher among those considered for admission and not hospitalized than it was among those admitted.[20]

These observations on the misuse of Section 29 are enough to warrant the concern that has been expressed within the last few years. Variations in administrative practice and attitudes with respect to compulsory admission are fairly dramatic. Even if allowance is made for such things as the use of Section 29 in order to avoid the waiting list for geriatrics,[21] it is clear that coercion is employed in many situations in which it is not necessary.

The Royal Commission on Mental Illness suggested that less than 5 percent of all admissions should have to be formal, and we noted earlier the widely quoted estimate that 90% of all mental hospital admissions in the country were voluntary. Yet the research to be cited below* found that the average percentage of voluntary admissions over a seven-year period was 81.3—leaving almost four times as many involuntary admissions as was deemed necessary by the Royal Commisssion. Furthermore, the proportion seems not to be increasing with time, although given the development of alternative services and psychotropic drugs one would expect a steadily decreasing proportion of involuntary admissions.

---
* Miller, Simons, and Fein.

National Variability in the Use of Compulsory Powers

The variability noted above, along with previously noted regional differences in the use of voluntary hospitalization going back over a number of years, raises questions about the British national experience with respect to all formal admissions under the Mental Health Act. Wide differences would indicate that factors other than the behavior of the individual are paramount in hospitalization decisions.

The following discussion of the use of compulsory hospitalization in England and Wales is based upon an analysis of admissions to designated mental hospitals from 1964 through 1970. Miller, Simons, and Fein reported and analyzed in detail variations in the use of compulsory powers between the fifteen regions of England and Wales, across time within regions, and by age, sex, and admission history.[22]

They found that three of these variables—region of the country, year, and age—explained 43 percent of the variation in legal status of the patient upon entry to the hospital. Age explained by far the greatest proportion of the variance, apparently owing to a policy or convention that young people are generally admitted informally. The proportion of variance explained by region and year is probably due in large measure to variations in policy in the different regions, and to changes in administrative emphasis from one year to another. These observations were confirmed when the youngest age group was omitted from the analysis, revealing stronger correlations between legal status and year, region, and sex. Younger people and females were more likely to have been admitted informally. Region explained considerably more variance than any other variable, supporting the argument that policy, official, or unofficial, is highly significant.

In short, the variability noted in the use of Section 29 of the Mental Health Act also exists at the national level when all sections of the act relating to formal admission are analyzed. Since there are no data to indicate that individuals or communities were worse off at these times and in those places where formal admissions were used relatively infrequently, it seems clear that compulsory powers are used much more frequently than is warranted.

Supportive evidence for this conclusion can be found in the work of Lawson.[23] She reported that many of the factors associated with compulsory admission were administrative in nature—e.g., availability of beds, length of waiting list, time of day, and age of patient. In a detailed study of patients admitted to the mental hospitals of Camberwell during 1970, Dawson raised the question of whether compulsion is at all necessary.[24] Through interviews with patients and those concerned with admitting patients, he compared groups of different admission status with respect to: burden or stress on the family, relatives' knowledge of services, fear of mental hospitals, social isolation, denial of illness, and disturbed (dangerous) behavior. The two groups were matched with respect to sex, diagnostic category, and approximate age; the only significant differences between the groups were with respect to willingness to enter the hospital and denial of illness. Dawson concluded that the various reasons given for admission failed to provide an explanation as to why compulsion was necessary; the only reason for coercion appeared to be that the patient did not agree that admission was necessary. Dawson further suggested that no improvement in psychiatric services would affect the use of compulsion, and that for any change in the use of compulsion to occur there would have to be a more tolerant attitude on the part of the general public and greater tolerance for those who have psychiatrically handicapped relatives. Once again, the significance of individual values was underscored. The variability noted in overall hospital admission rate (from 2.5/1,000 to 9/1,000 in 1969[25]) was also found to exist in the use of compulsion.

This discussion has dealt with coercion only as it is reflected in the use of formal hospitalization powers in an overt, direct manner. There can be no question that some of the people who were admitted involuntarily would have voluntarily entered and remained in the hospital. On the other hand, the very existence in law of compulsory powers serves as a significant threat, and there is reason to believe that the degree of operative coercion is much greater than is reflected in the figures on formal admission. In several hospitals in England I talked to admitting physicians and patients who acknowledged this point. If a physician says to an individual that he needs to be in the hospital and that he has a choice of entering in an informal status or having papers filed, most people will choose the former course. There are also other, less direct ways of keeping people in hospitals. Heavy sedation, particularly upon admission, is not uncommon, and not allowing the patient to wear his street clothes also has an inhibiting effect. The existence of both of these practices was confirmed to me by staff and patients.

An interesting perspective on voluntary hospital admission has been provided by four American psychiatrists writing about the British system. They make reference to the widespread use of voluntary admission to mental hospitals in England and then go on to say that local health officers attempt to persuade a patient who needs hospital care to go voluntarily. If he is hesitant or refuses, he is told that if he does not accept the option of voluntary admission he will be sent under observation status, thus endangering his civil rights. Most choose to go voluntarily.[26]

Aside from indicating that the degree of coercion is much higher than that reflected in official statistics, the writers seem to assume that "voluntary and free admission" has been achieved if the legal definition is met. Under these conditions, a mental hospital system could have only voluntarily admitted patients and yet not have a single patient who had willingly chosen to enter.

Appeals Against Commitment

With the passage of the 1959 Mental Health Act and the virtual abolition of judicial authority in the admission process, a need was recognized for an appeals process to protect against abuses. Review tribunals were established consisting of a lawyer, a doctor, and a lay member, with the lawyer as chairman. The tribunals were not empowered to consider the legality of the initial commitment or the adequacy of treatment; their only option was to order the patient discharged or to continue hospitalization.

In the first five years of operation of the appeals process there were 5,423 applications, with 12 percent of these patients receiving a discharge.[27] The figures for 1967–68 reflect a similar pattern. During this period there were 2,095 applications with 1,771 hearings held, and an overall discharge rate of 12 percent.[28] It is interesting to note that those who were given a formal hearing had a discharge rate almost double that of those cases which were heard informally (27 percent versus 14 percent). This is consistent with the general finding reported in the next chapter that formal hearings more frequently result in the individual avoiding hospitalization.

The provision for appeal against abuse of commitment is clearly an important one. But the figures suggest that only a small proportion of the formally admitted will leave the hospital by means of a successful appeal. Approximately 6 percent of those involuntarily admitted to hospitals make appeal and of these, 12 percent are discharged. What is not known is how many of the patients are aware of their right to appeal. From the evidence presented earlier in this chapter, one would expect that a careful appeals review would result in a higher release rate.

On the other hand, just as the existence of compulsory powers serves as a threat, it is probable that some patients gain release by threatening an appeal. That is, some physicians may alter the status of a patient rather than go through the time-consuming process of appearing as a witness in the review process.

FORCES FOR REFORM

Throughout British history there have been periodic organized reforms movements aimed at the asylums. As early as 1845 there was an organization called the *Alleged Lunatics Friends Society*. Within the last ten years the antipsychiatry and antihospitalization movement appears to have reached new heights. British journalists regularly call for reform, documenting the problems of overcrowding, understaffing, and abuse of patients. A government study released by the Department of Health and Social Security in 1971 refers to barnlike dormitories in which patients are herded together. One report notes that "padded rooms and a large number of locked wards are still in use in some hospitals."[29] The distinguished British medical journal *Lancet* notes a number of injustices in psychiatric hospitals, including the patient's loss of the right to have any say in treatment, the right to know what is happening to him, and the right to appeal against decisions made about him.[30]

The National Association for Mental Health has been conducting for some time what it refers to as the "Mind Campaign," which is particularly concerned with the rights of patients compulsorily detained under the various sections of the 1959 Mental Health Act.[31] The campaign notes that there are considerable differences between regions in the proportion of patients admitted compulsorily, prompting the suspicion we noted above that some patients are admitted under detention order because it is easier for the social worker or more convenient administratively. The campaign calls for issuance by the Department of Health of guidance on the rights of patients to refuse treatment, examination of procedures for the renewal of detention, and financial assistance for lay representation of patients at review tribunals. The association is concerned generally with upgrading the services provided for mental patients, but it is significant that it should focus specifically on the condition of the compulsorily detained.

Some particularly interesting material has been produced by the Society for Individual Freedom, an independent voluntary organization, generally conservative in outlook, concerned with national issues affecting individual liberty. In the summer of 1971, it established a committee of inquiry into compulsory psychiatric practices, which went about gathering a variety of facts, including instances of abuses against individuals. The focus was upon abuses in England and Wales, but inquiries were made abroad as well. In addition to sending questionnaires to individuals, governmental bodies, mental health professionals, and Members of Parliament, the committee solicited responses from the general public through the newspapers and television. At this writing, a final report of the committee's work has not yet been published, but having worked with this committee for several months I had the opportunity to review a number of the thousands of submitted questionnaires and responses from the general public.

The number of submissions was surprisingly high considering the limited publicity given the work of the committee. There can be no question but that many of the submissions came from confused, disturbed ex-patients whose claims were subject to some question. But it was equally clear that many of the reports were plausible, documented in considerable detail, and from reliable sources. Generalizations from this kind of information should be limited, but several trends are worth noting.

There were relatively few claims of violation of the law, but numerous complaints about the process itself. Ex-patients told of not being informed about where they were being taken or for how long; reference was made to depressions and suicidal impulses stemming from being compulsorily detained; there were complaints of a lack of control over one's own treatment; and, most importantly, there were a large number of reports of threats of compulsion in order to bring about ("voluntary") hospitalization. In addition, it is worth nothing that objections came not only from laymen but from several mental health professionals who argued for the abolition of all compulsory hospitalization. The unrest reflected in the creation of the committee of inquiry and likely to be intensified by the publication of the committee report may well lead to some modification of the Mental Health Act.

Considerable unrest over compulsory hospitalization exists on an international basis, with many European countries now having at least rudimentary organizations attempting to curtail or abolish the practice. And England now has a Mental Patients' Union, a voluntary association of present and former hospital patients.[32] A major objective of the group is to "expose the myth that most treatment and admission to mental hospitals is really 'voluntary' (as opposed to technically voluntary)" and to achieve the abolition of compulsory hospitalization.

SUMMARY AND OUTLOOK

In many respects the British system of health care and organization of psychiatric services is quite different from that operating in the United States. All but approximately 100 of the nation's psychiatrists are in the National Health Service, psychiatry is closely integrated with other medical specialties, and the analogy of psychiatric illness to physical illness is strongly made. With respect to psychiatric hospitalization, the procedure followed is entirely medical and there is a long history of concern with developing open hospitals and making compulsory admission an unlikely event.

Yet the British have forgotten their own recent history, which contains dramatic examples of the extent to which mental hospitals can successfully abolish physical restraint. Although the rhetoric is there, they have not come close to the stated goal of the rare use of compulsion in hospital admissions. Rather, coercion of some degree continues to be a relatively common event. Just as in the United States, there is marked variability in the use of compulsion and this seems to be due to administrative practice and attitudes rather than to differences in the distribution of mental illness. It is relatively easy to find examples of the use of hospitalization to resolve social problems, and in the words of one British psychiatrist,

> We know that as long as we have mental hospitals we are unlikely to prevent admission to them. Hopes that this would happen have always overlooked one important aspect of psychiatric care: the desire of mental health professionals to get rid of undesirable patients.[33]

All the evidence suggests that the British mental hospitals will continue to exist in the face of much talk about closing them. The Department of Health and Social Services has for some time estimated a decrease in the number of psychiatric beds needed, but the admission rate to mental hospitals continues to rise even as psychiatric services in district general hospitals have increased.[34] Again, this parallels the experience in the United States. Thus the conditions under which persons enter and leave the mental hospitals will continue to be of considerable significance. It will be interesting to see if the current unrest on the British scene will have a significant impact upon hospital admission practices or if a more radical impact will evolve from the legal attack being mounted in the United States.

6.

Involuntary Hospitalization: A Medical or a Legal Procedure?

"We haven't changed the commitment laws of France in thirty years. We just change our interpretation of them."

Pierre Jean

"The lawyer representing a prospective patient in a typical civil commitment proceeding is a stranger in a strange land without benefit of guidebook, map, or dictionary. Too often he shows no interest and makes no effort to learn his way about his foreign environment. As a result, free citizens of a free country are frequently deprived of their liberty for an indefinite duration."

Fred Cohen
Texas Law Review

THE AREA OF CIVIL COMMITMENT has been described as the battleground between medicine and law. Contrasting positions are reflected in statements put forth by national organizations representing the two professions. The Group for the Advancement of Psychiatry argues simply that involuntary hospitalization should occur upon certification by two physicians. Adjudication by a court would take place only when a patient petitioned for a writ of habeas corpus, and only after hospitalization had already been effected.[1] In contrast, the American Bar Association takes the position that any deprivation of liberty necessarily requires application of due-process procedures prior to hospitalization.[2]

These simple statements lay out the battle lines and can serve as starting points in elaborating the sources of conflict. The legal profession is concerned with constitutional issues and with ensuring that no one be deprived of liberty without due process. The guiding rule is the assumption of innocence, which with respect to civil commitment means an assumption that the client is not mentally ill. Psychiatry, like other medical specialties, operates under an opposite rule which says that when in doubt it is best to suspect or assume the presence of disease. Just as it is a serious error for an innocent person to be convicted, so is it a serious issue for a physician to fail to detect pathology when it is present. Thus the two professions start out with opposite orientations with respect to this issue.

They also differ with respect to the public versus private dimension of civil commitment. The law is primarily a public system with an emphasis upon due process, regardless of the inconvenience or discomfort suffered by the persons involved. In contrast, psychiatry is used to operating in private within the framework of the traditional doctor–patient relationship, and with a concern that the individual get help as quickly as possible with minimum embarrassment and discomfort. The formal requirements of court procedure and legal trappings—notice, hearings, cross-examination—are seen as unnecessary and harmful; they imply a moral failure on the part of the patient when it is sickness that is involved. Thus the legal process is seen not only as delaying treatment but also as stigmatizing. Furthermore, from the psychiatric perspective, when courts and attorneys get involved in determining the need for hospitalization they are encroaching upon an area that is outside of their competence. Hospital admission should be an administrative procedure followed at medical discretion; judicial review is unnecessary because there is no motive to detain unjustifiably, particularly since all hospitals already have more work than they can handle. Not so, says the attorney. In the first place, no one questions the right of the court to "butt in" in medical affairs—witness malpractice suits, the role of the court in workmen's compensation, and the determination of disability benefits. These are clearly medical issues, but there is a consensus that the court has a legitimate role to play in adjudicating them. Secondly, even though railroading into mental hospitals is assumed to be probably a very rare event these days and mental health professionals are by and large assumed to act in good faith, even the most conscientious person, it is assumed, may depart from the law on occasion and will need to be checked by the court.

There are other potential sources of conflict between attorneys and psychiatrists.[3] Psychiatrists are trained to microscopically scrutinize unusual behavior, with an emphasis upon mental illness and internal functioning. Lawyers are prone to place limits on the relevance of unusual behavior or thought, and to explain it away in terms of everyday experience. There is conflict over the purposes of hospitalization, with psychiatry not only concerned with the individual but often recommending hospitalization for the sake of the family or of society. The physician can argue that a mentally ill person cannot be expected to rationally decide if he needs hospitalization, whereas the attorney points out that it is the question of mental illness that the court needs to determine in the first place. And a different perspective is involved in the fact that the attorney, in contrast to the court and the psychiatrist, does not bear ultimate responsibility in decisions to hospitalize.

Several recent trends have sharpened the question of whether civil commitment should be a legal or a medical procedure. As was noted in Chapter I, there is now an organized movement of some significance that has as its aim the abolition of all forms of involuntary hospitalization for mental illness. The movement draws its strength from within the mental health professions as well as the law. A second thrust stems from recent court decisions on the right to treatment, jury awards for false imprisonment, and heightened concern with the civil rights of individuals who are deprived of their liberty under the *parens patriae* doctrine. Yet, at the same time, the state is in the process of expanding the number of people designated to receive forced treatment. Alcoholics, drug addicts, sexual offenders, and other troublesome people are being transferred from correctional to health care systems. State statutes relating to hospitalization and treatment are constantly under revision, usually reflecting attempts to combine legal and medical features.[4]

It is clear that there are grounds for conflict between law and psychiatry over the manner in which involuntary hospitalization should occur. But the real question is whether there is, in fact, a substantial conflict. Is the supposed battle restricted to the pages of learned journals and specially arranged symposia? What role does the court in fact play in commitment proceedings? Is due process a reality? Are there facts to help us decide how the commitment process should operate? We turn now to the evidence which speaks to these questions. Policy recommendations are offered where appropriate throughout the chapter.

HOSPITALIZATION AS A LEGAL PROCEDURE

Aside from basic questions about the constitutionality of the law of civil commitment as it exists on the books, there are more important questions about the law in action. To the extent that civil commitment is in fact a legal proceeding involving due process, we would expect the following conditions to hold:

- Provision of formal notice would be made to the alleged incompetent.
- A speedy and full hearing would be held in the presence of the alleged incompetent, who would have the right to face accusers and cross-examine them.
- Attorneys playing an adversary role would be frequently involved.
- Hearsay evidence would be excluded.
- The individual would have the right to remain silent during all commitment proceedings.
- Notice would be given of the right to trial by jury.
- The court-appointed examining committee would submit careful and detailed evaluations.

- There would frequently be contradictory evidence and recommendations (given the widely acknowledged variations in the definition and judgment of what constitutes mental illness and the ease with which experts holding contradictory opinions can be found).
- The judgment process (in such a complicated and ambiguous area) would take some time.
- The court would on occasion come to a judgment contrary to the recommendations of the examining physicians.
- Statutory specificity regarding the requirements for commitment would obtain.
- The burden of proving the defendant mentally ill and dangerous would rest upon the state.
- Proof beyond a reasonable doubt would be required.[5]

Notice

The requirement that notice be given has been described by a psychiatrist as "the most infuriating of the legal features of commitment."[6] This response is usually based upon concern that the patient may flee, kill himself, be prompted to violence against another, or suffer psychological harm. A candid response from one hospital administrator is less complicated: "I don't give a damn about the patient's civil rights—as a doctor. Our job is healing people, and assisting the court to do its job."[7]

A further argument against giving notice is that it is an ineffective step—it does not affect ultimate outcome and most of the people involved are incapable of taking advantage of the notice. The counterargument has been expressed by the Kansas Court of Appeals:

> Notice and opportunity to be heard lie at the foundation of all judicial procedures. They are fundamental

principles of justice which cannot be ignored. . . . it will not do to say that it is useless to serve notice upon an insane person, that it would avail nothing because of his inability to take advantage of it. His sanity is the very thing to be tried.[8]

The American Bar Association is also clear on its position regarding notice:

Any person, before he is committed to a mental hospital, or otherwise deprived of his liberty, should be served with notice and given a full opportunity to be heard.[9]

Although the United States Supreme Court has recognized that notice that is reasonably calculated to apprise one of the pendency of an action against him is a fundamental requirement of due process,[10] notice has not, surprisingly, been uniformly required by the courts in mental incompetency proceedings.[11] But if the issue gets contested, it seems likely that decisions will be similar to a 1972 ruling in a federal district court that a prospective patient must be given notice and information beyond the time and place of a hearing. In order to facilitate a defense, the order required that the notice contain the reasons for detention, the identities of those who will testify at the hearing, and the probable content of their testimony.[12]

Currently only one-half of the states require such notice.[13] An additional twelve states require that notice be given unless this procedure is judged to be potentially harmful to the individual. For those states that require notice, there is little evidence regarding how the requirement works in practice, and what evidence there is suggests that the law is not taken very seriously. A study of five years of activity in a Florida county revealed that in many instances there was no record on file that a notice had been served or signed by anyone.[14] Even when notice is served not much protection for the individual is involved, since Florida law provides for the notice to be signed by any person over the age of 14 living in the household of the person for whom the notice is intended; the lack of protection becomes apparent when one realizes that in 70 to 80 percent of the cases it is a family member who initiates the proceedings. The absurdity of this procedure insofar as the protection of civil rights is concerned is further brought out by the fact that signing the acceptance of the notice usually involved waiving the right to a hearing. In over seven hundred incompetency proceedings in the Florida study mentioned above, 64 percent of the notices sent were in fact signed by a relative.

Some courts have reasoned that due-process defects stemming from failure to give notice would be cured by subsequent review or appeal provisions.[15] But this reasoning does not acknowledge that the review process may come into play only after a relatively severe deprivation of liberty. Even in California, a state whose laws on hospitalization reflect a strong concern for civil rights, a person can be involuntarily hospitalized for thirty-three days on the signature of one physician.

The timing of a notice is also of significance, since the purpose of the notice is to allow the alleged incompetent an opportunity to prepare for a hearing. Several states specify that twenty-four hours is sufficient notice—hardly enough time in which to seek assistance or prepare much of a defense.[16] A two-hour interval has been considered reasonable notice for a violent person.[17] An indication of the current trend to deemphasize the significance of notice and hearing is the total elimination of these provisions from the New York State statutes.[18]

If the commitment proceeding is to provide due process, as we have argued that it should, then clearly the issuance of notice is essential. This should hold even though it is probable that at the time of consideration of hospitalization many people are not in a state to remember or understand the notice.[19] The provision of notice entails minimal expense to the state and could make a difference to some individuals.

RECOMMENDATION

Notice of the time and place of a commitment hearing should be mandatory, should be given in sufficient time to allow preparation of a defense, and should provide essential details of the alleged grounds for detention. The notice should be given directly to the prospective patient.

Hearing

A mandatory hearing is called for in all but two states. But just as with the notice of a hearing, this right is frequently waived, ignored, or in some way left to the discretion of the court. Hearings are thus relatively rare and nearly always of a *pro forma* nature when they are held. The patient is usually not present and has not been observed by the judge, and there is very little in the way of a serious attempt to elicit information or determine facts as in other types of legal hearings. These observations have been made a number of times and can now be supported by systematic studies of thousands of cases in widely different settings.[20] In many courts the proceedings are not bound by the rules of evidence; no transcript is made and rarely is an appeal taken.[21]

That the hearing provides only an illusion of due process is brought home when its typical length is considered. A review of the studies noted above reveals that the average time consumed in involuntary hospitalization hearings is less than five minutes, and it is not at all uncommon for the mean time to be below two minutes. (An average hearing time of sixteen minutes reported in one New York study is extremely high. This may be due in part to the fact that these hearings came after hospitalization.[22]) It is clear that decisions have been made at some other point in the process and that the hearing is ceremonial rather than functional. The filing of a petition virtually ensures commitment.

In many respects civil commitment hearings are analogous to juvenile court proceedings: nonadversary, civil, concerned with helping rather than punishing, and generally adjudicating personal status rather than proof of an act. Although recent court decisions have underscored the unconstitutionality of many juvenile court procedures and safeguards have been instituted, the same has not occurred with respect to civil commitment.

RECOMMENDATION

There should be a mandatory hearing in all civil commitment cases, with the prospective patient present and having the right to cross-examine witnesses and call witnesses on his own behalf. Funds should be available to pay the fees of a psychiatrist testifying for the prospective patient. It is probably advisable to hold the hearing in the same setting where other civil matters are heard. A hearing held with the patient already in the hospital could influence the decision, in that the setting might convey the suggestion that hospitalization is called for.[23]

The Involvement of Attorneys

The right to counsel, constitutionally derived under the sixth and fourteenth amendments, has been widely recognized as a basic procedural safeguard. Although the Supreme Court has not spoken on the constitutional right to counsel in civil commitment proceedings, other federal courts have.[24] A number of states now provide this right in involuntary hospitalization proceedings, but less than half make such provisions in all cases.[25] In many instances the right is merely a permission and there are no provisions for compensation. For these and other reasons to be described below, attorneys are rarely involved. A national study supported by the American Bar Association documented this fact in considerable detail.[26] For example, private attorneys are involved in only 3 of 202 cases studied in Kansas and in less than one out of twenty in Los Angeles. Similar experiences have been reported from other states.[27]

Even when counsel is guaranteed the alleged incompetent, he frequently ends up not represented.[28] Attorneys are reluctant to get involved in incompetency proceedings, and situations are not structured so to encourage their participation. In instances where a person is permitted to call a lawyer, lists of lawyers are not available and referral and legal aid arrangements have not been established. Several authors report a general tendency on the part of mental health professionals to discourage the raising of legal questions, on the assumption that the result would be increased stress for the patient. Again, the expectation conveyed is that all of the people involved will behave responsibly and that a medical problem such as mental illness should not be referred to a court.

In those rare instances when an attorney is involved in the commitment process, he is frequently silent and essentially roleless.[29] Cohen argues that this is so because the proceedings are defined as nonadversary, and the adversary role is the only one in which the lawyer is trained.

> . . . the lawyer involved in a civil commitment case has no tradition to rely upon, develops no experience in this area because of a limited number of appearances, has little in his professional training to prepare him for this role, and has no source to consult for guidance; also, the county judge is unlikely to require any more than a perfunctory performance.[30]

His appointment, then, is usually in compliance with a formal requirement and ends up being only a formality. Frequently he remains mute (except for checking to see if signatures are in order on the appropriate forms) and has not communicated with his client or investigated the events which brought about the hearing. An extreme example of this phenomenon comes from observation of indefinite-commitment hearings in Travis County, Texas:

> The attorney, in accordance with the normal practice, had been appointed to represent all the patients whose hearings were scheduled that day. While awaiting the opening of the hearings, the writer asked the attorney how many cases were to be heard that day. "Forty, I believe." "Have you contacted any of the proposed patients?" "No, I haven't but I did receive letters from two of them. I may get a chance to consult with them before we get under way." That opportunity did not materialize. This was the attorney's first appointment as attorney ad litem and, to put it most kindly, he was somewhat uncertain about his function.[31]

Where a public defender is involved, the situation is even more ambiguous. Who is the client: the state or the individual? The problematics involved are summarized in the following statement by a public defender interviewed in the Brakel and Rock study:

> When a public defender finds himself in this situation he is put in the position of playing "God." The humane thing for him to do is to yield in cases in which he feels the patient is actually ill. While I feel my role as an advocate, I also feel a moral responsibility for the welfare of the patient. I do not feel that I am really qualified to judge whether a person is mentally ill and then, on the basis of this personal analysis, to defend him either strenuously or half-heartedly, yet I am constantly called upon to make just this determination and do in fact make it. My personal judgments do affect my defense of a patient. I do not like being put in this position. It is just too much responsibility on the public defender's shoulders.[32]

There are some situations in which the individual might hope that his attorney would remain passive, for the suggestion has been made that the attorney himself may on occasion have been the one to have initiated incompetency proceedings.

> If you feel you cannot persuade the client himself to get help, perhaps it is your professional responsibility to initiate the process. But you may well want to keep your own role a permanent secret from the client, although this would involve continuing the duplicity even after the latter's sanity returns.[33]

This is an extreme example, but it is consistent with an analysis of civil commitment practices in New York which led to the conclusion that in many cases the lawyer not infrequently assumed the position of judge rather than advocate.[34]

What happens in those rare instances when an attorney plays an advocate role? The evidence is somewhat skimpy but highly consistent: it *does* make a difference. Rock and his colleagues reported on the basis of their observations in Kansas that when any serious legal question was raised the state immediately dropped its case. Wenger and Fletcher found that even in a situation in which the patient's condition was held constant, the introduction of legal counsel strongly influenced the probability of release; they report a correlation of .94 between the presence of a lawyer and being released rather than hospitalized.[35] The potential significance of the attorney is also reflected in a study of court activity in Lancaster County, Nebraska. In about a third of the cases where the "accused" was represented the result was dismissal or continuance; this compared with 12 dismissals out of 188 cases in which the "accused" did not have counsel.[36] Even the presence of non-attorney observers at commitment courts may bring about a decrease in the likelihood of commitment. When observers from the California Mental Health Association were present at commitment hearings, only 43 percent of the persons brought before the court were committed, as compared with 76 percent the preceding month, when observers were not present.[37]

RECOMMENDATION

The appointment of an attorney should be mandatory and should occur immediately after an application is filed and the person is taken into custody. It should be understood that the attorney's role is adversarial, and he should be present at psychiatric exams and actively involved at all stages in presenting the available alternatives to his client.

Jury Trial

Trial by jury is a rare occurrence in commitment proceedings, and the courts have not uniformly held that such a right is constitutionally required. Some of the disadvantages of a jury trial are fairly obvious. Jury trials are time-consuming, expensive to the state, and more formal than other procedures. It has been suggested that attorneys rarely request a jury trial because most patients would be released by the time the trial took place, the process could be disturbing to the patient, and a jury would come to the same decision as a judge anyhow. All of these arguments have some merit, but they are outweighed by advantages which may be less obvious.

For one thing, the very existence of the possibility of a jury trial may cause the court to take its role as a fact finder more seriously and apply due-process requirements more stringently. It is also likely that in the desire to avoid jury trials there would be more negotiated releases and a more careful consideration of the need for commitment in each individual case. Probably of still greater importance is that a jury trial introduces community values into the decision-making process and elevates societal judgments to a position of primacy. The judgment of the individual's peers is interposed between the state (and/or one or more physicians) and the individual, making arbitrary commitments more difficult.

A jury trial should be mandatory upon the request of the individual or his attorney, and it should be required that the prospective patient be informed of his statutory right to a jury trial. The second part of this recommendation is crucial, since the tendency is to ignore this right or discourage its use.

The Right to Remain Silent

The privilege against self-incrimination has long been considered to be a vital aspect of due process, and a federal district court has ruled that an individual cannot be committed on the basis of information gathered from a psychiatric examination unless he has knowledge of his right to refuse to answer questions.[38] In light of the unreliability of diagnostic interviews and the invasion of privacy involved, this would appear to be an obvious protection to be offered the individual, although it impairs the state's ability to commit.

RECOMMENDATION

In commitment proceedings the individual should have the right to refuse to answer questions.

Court and Examining Committee Congruence

Much attention has been given to the infringement of civil liberties resulting from various institutional psychiatric practices, but little has been said about the failure of the courts to ensure fair judicial review.[38] The evidence consistently indicates that in civil commitment proceedings the norm is for the court to defer to expert opinion.

If the assumption is made that the role of the court is to seek information, weigh evidence, and come to differential decisions, we would expect it to occasionally differ from the recommendation made by the examining committee. To the extent that the court simply endorses or rubber-stamps the recommendation of the committee, then the process is clearly medical rather than legal. From the evidence already presented in this chapter it will come as no surprise to learn that independent behavior on the part of the courts is rare. In the Rock et al. study, which involved the observation of over five hundred cases in Chicago, there were no discrepancies between the doctors' recommendations and a commission finding for or against commitment. The same was true of their observations in Los Angeles. Fein and Miller, studying a Florida court, found only two instances in over seven hundred decisions in which the adjudication differed from the examining committee recommendation. In both of these cases there were unusual circumstances suggesting that the judge did not disagree with the committee's recommendation but decided against it for other reasons (in one of the cases the person was declared competent so as to facilitate returning to his native country).[40] Wenger and Fletcher also report total congruence between judge and committee in the 81 cases they observed.[41] The literature contains a number of less systematic observations which are consistent with these studies, and only one report could be found which indicates any degree of independence on the part of the court. In an urban Florida community, the judge disagreed with the recommendations of the examining committee approximately 8 percent of the time.[42] In the majority of cases in which there were differences it was in the direction of the judge declaring the person incompetent against a committee recommendation of competence. From other observations it seems probable that this particular judge was conservative in outlook and felt that it was better to err in the direction of hospitalization.

The circumstances which lead courts to agree with examining committee recommendations have been succinctly described by David Mechanic:

> Since judges often are extremely busy and they usually assume that [mental] patients are likely to require detention and treatment, many consider it pointless to spend much time on a meticulous examination of each case. Most persons considered for commitment are eccentric and bizarre in appearance and manner. Thus almost invariably some evidence indicates that the "patient" is not an ordinary person. The difference between the "patient" and an ordinary man is often exaggerated by his being an "accused" person, in that others seek to find peculiarities which they can attribute to "mental illness." The judge himself usually has only a limited knowledge of mental illness, and he is unlikely to make subtle distinctions in evaluating the mental state of persons whose cases are presented to him. Even if he is not busy and has time to make a full investigation, he frequently fails to do so since he has faith in the medical model and is likely to depend on the opinions of the physicians appointed to examine the patient. The judge tends to define the physician as an expert in a matter in which he is at best only an amateur, and he is ordinarily reluctant to reject medical advice. Thus, if the medical examiners recommend

commitment, the judge may not hold a serious hearing; he may not conceive that he would allow his own observations to countermand the assessment of the medical examiners. With this frame of reference, it is in the interests neither of the alleged patient nor of the court to hold an extensive hearing. The court has other business to attend to and judges frequently assume that a legal hearing would not be conducive to the patient's mental health. Thus the commitment process has the form of due process of law but is actually vacuous since the decision tends to be predetermined.[43]

Recommendation

A simple correction to ensure that the court attend to the facts presented before it would be to require a statement by the court of the grounds for its findings. *The courts should be required to make findings of fact and conclusions of law for each civil commitment case.*

Committee Composition

Most states are quite specific in defining the composition of the examining committee. For example, Florida statutes require that the committee be composed of two physicians who are not professionally associated and an independent layman. Further stipulations are that the layman may not be employed by one of the examining physicians, that a person petitioning for the hearing may not serve on the committee, and that all committee members must sign the committee report. From earlier research we had reason to believe that many of these procedural safeguards were being ignored. In a review of five years of mental incompetency proceedings in a single court, we found that this was in fact the case, with 39 percent of the committees not meeting the legal requirements for one or more reasons.[44] This raised the question of whether having a legal committee made a difference in the final determination. The correlation between committee legality and adjudication was .21; persons with a legal committee were more likely to be declared competent. We have no reason to believe that there were any deliberate evasions of the law, but once again there is confirmation that the legal aspects of hospitalization are not taken very seriously.

Similar conclusions were drawn by Pfrender as a result of studying 221 habeas-corpus petitions at Kalamazoo State Hospital.[45] One hundred and ninety-eight petitions resulted in release because of imperfections in the way they were originally admitted. This is consistent with our earlier observation that the law relating to the criteria of dangerousness is generally ignored.

It is unlikely that violations in committee composition and other minor technical provisions have a major impact on the outcome of commitment proceedings, but adherence to the law would seem to be desirable. Systematic adherence to all pertinent safeguards would make it more difficult to stray from any one of them.

RECENT COURT DECISIONS

Broad changes in the law are usually brought about by legislation, but decisional or case law can also be a significant force for change. A series of court decisions within the last three to five years has probably had more effect on the law of civil commitment than all of the legislative change within the last thirty years. The most significant of these decisions stemmed from the right-to-treatment concept, first articulated in 1960 by Morton Birnbaum,[46] a concept which has increasingly been acknowledged as a constitutional right. The issue has been extensively litigated and has been the subject of a number of books, articles, and reviews.[47] Many of the major issues were noted in the discussion of the Donaldson case in Chapter 2, and only an outline of the subject needs to be mentioned here.

Simply put, the argument is that when the state involuntarily incarcerates someone solely because he is sufficiently mentally ill to require institutionalization, treatment must be provided. In some states this right is based on statutory provisions, frequently with the qualification that the right is restricted to the extent that funds and facilities are available. The constitutional basis for the right to treatment is found in the due-process and equal-protection-of-the-laws provisions of the fourteenth amendment, along with the eighth-amendment prohibition of cruel and unusual punishment. The reasoning is that since civil commitment of a mentally handicapped person is analogous to punishing him for his sickness, this is a violation of the eighth amendment. The general overcrowding and physical deprivation encountered in so many state institutions is interpreted as constituting cruel and unusual punishment.

The right to treatment was first considered judicially in 1966 in the case of Rouse v. Cameron in the United States Court of Appeals for the District of Columbia.[48] Rouse was charged with carrying a dangerous weapon and found not guilty by reason of insanity and committed to St. Elizabeth's Hospital. At the time of his court appearance he had been in the hospital for four years when the maximum sentence for the crime with which he was charged was one year. The court was confronted with the question of inadequate treatment and remanded the case to a district court for a factual hearing on that issue. The issue was never determined since Rouse was released for other reasons, but a number of other cases have developed since then. Not all jurisdictions have recognized the right-to-treatment doctrine, and even in those that have there has been limited implementation. But the number of such suits is expanding rapidly, and they encompass not only those who are committed as mentally ill under civil statutes but juveniles, sexual psychopaths, and other offenders as well.

We have already considered the findings in the appeal of Kenneth Donaldson, wherein the district court clearly supported the right-to-treatment doctrine. Probably the most significant class-action suit to date is that of Wyatt v. Stickney (later changed to Wyatt v. Aderholt), which was brought on behalf of patients at three Alabama institutions for the mentally disabled.[49] The Wyatt court assumed that the only constitutionally permissible justification for civil commitment was treatment and that failure to provide adequate treatment violated the fundamentals of due process. The court entered very specific orders, including requirements relating to the number and kind of additional employees to be hired, the frequency with which bed linens had to be changed, the opportunity for social contact with the opposite sex, etc. The state was given six months to institute a meaningful treatment program, and since then a number of improvements have occurred. But they are far short of the court's stipulations, and the financial problems seem insurmountable. Three years after the court ruling the mandated staffing ratios for professional categories have not been achieved and the institutions have not met the court's standards regarding individualized treatment plans.[50]

In Burnham v. Department of Public Health, the court held that the treatment of involuntary patients in mental hospitals was not an issue capable of definition and resolution by the courts.[51] This interpretation was later opposed by several other court decisions which held that the court can certainly review basic standards and see that appropriate expertise is brought into play.[52] Burnham v. Department of Mental Health was subsequently consolidated with Wyatt v. Aderholt, and thus the issue of the capability of the court to define treatment[53] was settled with the affirmation of Wyatt.

Along with the increased attention being given to the right to treatment, there is a beginning interest in the right to refuse treatment. Although judicial acceptance of this latter right has not been clearly established, several recent cases support it.[54] In light of the questionable effectiveness of treatment for mental illness and the goal of restricting coercion at every possible point, the right to refuse psychiatric treatment is basic, and as valid as the widely recognized right to refuse treatment for physical illness.

An additional doctrine which has grown out of the right-to-treatment cases is that of the use of the least restrictive alternative. The essential meaning of this doctrine is that a person should not be institutionalized until all alternative, less restrictive treatment approaches have been considered. Not only is the right to be treated in a setting less restrictive than an institution based on therapeutic considerations, but it is also derived from the constitutional principles of "the least drastic means." The constitution requires that whenever a government is going to restrict a person's liberty against his will in order to accomplish a governmental objective it must impose the least drastic restriction possible to accomplish this objective. Again, the courts have not been consistent on this point, but the trend has been to give the doctrine increased importance.[55] Constitutional issues aside, the use of alternative facilities is probably more effective than institutionalization, less expensive, and less disruptive of the patient's normal ties to the community.[56]

Several recent decisions question the state's authority to operate under the doctrine of *parens patriae,* particularly when the individual has not been declared incompetent.[57] The assumption that commitment is constitutional if attended by procedural safeguards is not in question, since it is recognized that a mentally ill person who is not dangerous cannot be deprived of his liberty if he retains the capacity to exercise judgment concerning the need for treatment. The major meaning of recent decisions on this issue has been that the court is now recognizing that justice will not be done by saying that a mental patient is a ward of the state and the state is acting only in his best interest. A determination of commitment is now being seen as no different from any other legal determination. In this context, a recent Wisconsin decision to the effect that involuntary mental commitment proceedings may not follow less stringent procedural standards than criminal proceedings reflects a further decline in the standing of the *parens patriae* doctrine.[58]

Still another tightening up of the standards governing commitment proceedings is reflected in recent decisions regarding preponderance-of-the-evidence vs. proof-beyond-a-reasonable-doubt grounds for commitment. In 1972, a Wisconsin statute was determined to be unconstitutional because it permitted a judge or a jury to commit a person on preponderance-of-the-evidence grounds; and in a second case a United States Court of Appeals affirmed that proof-beyond-a-reasonable-doubt criteria must be employed in civil commitments. In ruling that the highest possible procedural safeguards are compellingly necessary, the court said:

> The justifications for institutional confinement as a means of implementing state interests—in traditional terms retribution, deterrence and protection—are only partially applicable to civil commitment. The evidence which serves as a prerequisite to hospitalization remains uncertain . . . and the ultimate decision may therefore unduly reflect clinical, rather than the appropriate legal and community, considerations.[59]

A detailed discussion of the implications of using one or the other of these criteria can be found in an article by Charles Combs and in a recent issue of the *Harvard Law Review*.[60] Combs not only deals with the burden-of-proof question but also discusses the issue of vagueness in civil commitment proceedings. There seems to be no question but that due process would compel the invalidation of vague commitment statutes on the grounds that they invite arbitrary and discriminatory enforcement by officials.

Recommendations

Several specific recommendations can be drawn from the above discussion of recent court decisions:

1. *A patient should be allowed to refuse treatment.*
2. *The standard of proof in civil commitment should be proof beyond a reasonable doubt.*
3. *Restraint should always involve the principle of the least restrictive setting.*

In general there has been a trend to make civil commitment a more relaxed and less technical, quasi-judicial, and administrative procedure. Most of the recent court decisions mentioned above run counter to this trend and call for increased attention to traditional legal procedures. However, as we noted with respect to the right-to-treatment doctrine, these decisions have not generally been picked up in other jurisdictions and many of them have not moved up through higher court review.

A second and more important point has to do with the general distinction between law in action versus law as it exists on the books. As Ralph Slovenko has pointed out, laws are not self-executing and attorneys are no more interested in rendering service to people in mental hospitals than they are with respect to people in prisons, for there is little financial reward.[61] He goes on to suggest that laws are ignored because they are too complicated for the layman to comprehend, and in his judgment many of their features are unnecessary. The people who administer the commitment laws—hospital administrators, physicians, nurses, etc.—are not familiar with the laws on commitment although they are supposedly governed by them.

Even large-scale projects, thoughtfully drafted and enacted in major revisions of mental health codes, may have limited impact. A recent research report from the George Washington University Institute of Law, Psychiatry, and Criminology revealed that most of the reforms thought to have been effected several years earlier had been thwarted and frustrated in practice. Similarly, if court decisions such as those reviewed here are to achieve their potential in bringing about change, there enforcement will have to be carefully monitored.

Current Assessment

In the United States we have already gone through several periods in which attitudes toward involuntary hospitalization were distinctly different. Curran has suggested that the period after the Civil War up to about World War II could be described as "the romance with the criminal law."[62] During this period individuals being considered for involuntary hospitalization were given the protection of criminal procedural safeguards, and a major, guiding concern was that of avoiding railroading anyone into an insane asylum. This period was then followed by one described by Curran as "the romance with psychiatry," in which mental illness was defined solely as a medical problem and only the medical expert was involved in hospitalization decisions. Little attention was given to the legal aspects of entry into the hospital, but there was some beginning interest in providing for periodic review. Curran goes on to note that we are now into a third phase, "the disenchantment": viz, a disenchantment with punitive legal barriers and with excessive reliance on psychiatric judgment. As I have indicated in this chapter, there is evidence of a growing disenchantment, but it is not coming on with anything like a deafening roar. An excellent summary of this position grew out of an American Bar Foundation study:

> The judicial commitment procedure thus amounts to administrative monitoring, often cursory, of a medically oriented process upon which jural apparatus has been grafted. Under these conditions the court becomes essentially ministerial. The judge has neither the objective legal criteria nor the technical training to de-

cide the treatment questions that are really at stake. As a result, he is often reduced to deciding such ancillary administrative questions as what hospital the patient should be sent to, or passing on such procedural trivialities as the form of medical certificates. The medical treatment questions are determined by medical testimony from examiners whose opinions are rarely at variance and are rarely disputed. The court decides the central issues indirectly through the choice of medical examiners, a matter in which it has no special competence and for which it is not responsible to anyone.[63]

In light of this statement, it is not surprising that a member of the United States Supreme Court found it remarkable that the substantive constitutional limitations on the states' power to commit have not been more frequently litigated.[64] The Supreme Court has decided only four cases in its entire history dealing with any aspect of civil commitment, and two of these, and possibly a third, reflect primarily the concern of the court for persons convicted of crimes.[65]

In summary, conflict between the law and psychiatry over civil commitment proceedings is not substantial. The process is essentially medical, as a number of people feel that it should be. On the other hand, there is a small but growing demand that the illusion of due process must be corrected and that the same rights guaranteed to accused criminals and juveniles must be extended to people facing involuntary hospitalization. Recent court decisions have tended to support this movement by arguing that criminal and civil proceedings should not be substantially different because the end of both is essentially the same.

7.

Possibilities of Reform

THE EVIDENCE that has been reviewed argues strongly that involuntary hospitalization is an arbitrary process which primarily serves institutional purposes rather than the welfare of the individual, occurs much more frequently than is necessary, and does very little in the way of protecting either society or the individual. In addition, the consensus is that informal or voluntary admission is much to be preferred, and there have been predictions that by 1970 this would be the usual route of entry to state mental hospitals.[1] This goal has not been achieved because the forces of resistance are surprisingly strong. We noted that England has never approached its anticipated figure of less than 5 percent formal admissions. And the experience of the state of Florida is typical of the United States. Florida completely revised its mental health laws in 1971, with a major goal being the reduction of involuntary admissions. The data from its largest hospital revealed that in the first month of operation of the law the percentage of voluntary admissions rose from 9 percent to 72 percent, a dramatic shift. Yet one year later this proportion was back down to 35 percent.[2] Why is it so difficult to bring about change? What forces support a practice that seems to be so obviously undesirable? What needs to happen in order for significant reform to occur?

SOURCES OF RESISTANCE

Support for continued use of involuntary hospitalization comes in part out of a lack of familiarity with the evidence. Judges, hospital administrators, and physicians have not, for the most part, been exposed to the evidence presented in this book. There is little in their training that would sensitize them to the issues, and critical questions have begun to surface only within the last few years.

But lack of exposure to the evidence is only part of the problem. Differential interpretations of that evidence are also of significance. Just as there are those who still do not believe that the evidence of Watergate implicates former President Nixon, there are mental health professionals who do not believe in the validity of current findings relating to involuntary hospitalization. Certainly a majority of clinicians seem to believe that they can predict dangerousness with greater accuracy than the objective evidence suggests, just as they have more faith in the efficacy of hospitalization and treatment than is warranted.

There is also the fear that people will not go to the hospital willingly, and that if they do they may not stay for maximum benefit. The argument is that many patients lack insight, and thus by definition their judgment with respect to accepting or declining treatment is faulty. Since they do not know what is in their best interests, the argument goes, involuntary admission is necessary.

It is interesting to note that the people who argue against abolishing involuntary hospitalization like to point out that many patients willingly enter hospitals and that most admissions are noncontested. Reference is made to Veterans Administration hospitals, with their waiting lists of people begging for admission, and the argument is developed in the following manner:

> Further development of pharmacological drugs, community-based programs and involvement of a larger segment of the public will cause civil commitment laws to be regarded as an archiac vestige of a bygone era. In this day of open wards, close hospital–community liaison, frequent patient leaves of absence, and volunteer workers moving in and out of all psychiatric wards, the kinds of fears prompting legalistic provisions are becoming increasingly out of place.[3]

The millennium is seen as on the way if not already here, and in a puzzled way these people want to know what all the noise is about. Aside from questions that can be raised about the validity of such observations, it is remarkable that people holding this perspective are unable to see the contradictions inherent in their continuing to argue for involuntary commitment.

To all of these factors can be added the general resistance to organizational change. For years the way to enter a mental hospital has been as an involuntary patient, and this has served the purposes of the hospital well. Clerks, judges, family physicians, and admitting officers at a hospital find it easier to continue doing the familiar and safe thing. Professional organizations, as would be expected, have done very little to encourage critical appraisal and consequent change.

For example, in 1972 the board of trustees of the American Psychiatric Association expressed concern over allegations that psychiatrists employed by the government (in schools, hospitals, prisons, and the military) often served the interests of the institution rather than those of the patient, and thus functioned as instruments of social control.[4] The trustees appointed an *ad hoc* committee to study the use of psychiatric institutions for the commitment of political dissenters, with the understanding that the major focus was to be upon the Soviet Union, where numerous abuses had surfaced. The appointment of the committee was in part a response to the failure of the International Psychiatric Congress to take any action in 1971. The charge to the committee was eventually expanded to include American psychiatry, a staff was hired, and grant support was obtained for a major study. But soon after work started the trustees began having second thoughts, and the study was scuttled. The committee disbanded amid charges from the trustees that the study was too broad, unscientific, and biased by the choice of field researchers (two former Nader's Raiders). Now, after several years, the association may have evolved a formula that will allow such a study to go ahead.[5] No one anticipates a very critical analysis.

The American Psychological Association has finally begun talking about moving on the issue. In 1974, its Council of Representatives called for an exploration of the necessity and feasibility of a study within the United States of the practice of suppressing and neutralizing political dissenters by diagnosing them as mentally ill and committing them to mental hospitals. The resolution called for the American Psychological Association's representatives to the Assembly of the International Union of Psychological Science to take up the question of conducting an international survey. But as with the American Psychiatric Association, there has been no rush to implement such an investigation. The Executive Committee of the International Union of Psychological Science decided in a closed session not to sponsor such a study.[6]

It is reasonable to assume that some combination of the factors mentioned above must be operating to sustain involuntary hospitalization, with lack of familiarity with the evidence probably the most important. No one involved seems to know much about the process of hospitalization and it remains mysterious and confusing. But at the same time there is a more serious issue: the readiness, especially in times of conflict, to err on the side of protecting society as opposed to protecting the individual. The demands on the mental health system to deal with troublesome people of all sorts are increasing, and hospitalization is one way of managing a segment of these people. Communities and courts are unhappy with early release programs and over the apparent ease with which people leave mental hospitals. The desire is for social order; the pressure is to restrain people. The tendency is to be far more sensitive to the inconvenience, distraction, and discomfort caused by peculiar people than to their right to be different and to the qualities which they share in common with "normal" people. This philosophy is reflected in the following observation by a prominent psychiatrist, Leopold Bellak, on the need for public health laws for psychiatric illness:

The further invasion of individual rights and liberty is regrettable; all possible safeguards should be instituted. But the principle involved—and the consequences—are not different from other regulatory practices which are tolerated because they seem to be vital.[7]

Two aspects of this remark deserve comment. First, it is premised on a faith in technical competency. That is, Bellak believes that we can agree on who is psychiatrically ill and he has faith in the effectiveness of treatment—assumptions open to question. Secondly, it demonstrates that psychiatry serves primarily the state and not the individual, and that therapeutic technology is easily employed for social control. Under the mental health laws we are willing to readily commit, whereas under criminal law we are theoretically willing to let a hundred guilty men go free rather than wrong one innocent person. At least Bellak is overt in laying out his position, and the important issue here is that the mental health professional involved in commitment proceedings should acknowledge to himself and to the patient that his primary loyalty is to the state. This use of hospitalization for the maintenance of social order has not been widely acknowledged, and only recently have we begun to realize that mental health proceedings can be used to remove or neutralize bothersome persons.

The balance is continuing to shift, in that there is a growing feeling that the most fundamental right of the patient is the right to adequate treatment, and that this should take precedence over an absolute right to liberty. There is concern about the right of families to not have "a seriously disturbed and untreated patient residing in the household" as well as a concern that the patient ". . . be helped to take his place in society and comfortably."[8] The abolition or tightening of commitment laws would make these objectives more difficult of attainment.

Probably the most arrogant and inappropriate reasons for continuing involuntary hospitalization have been put forth in editorial comments in the *Psychiatric Quarterly*. The editor is critical of the New York Mental Hygiene Law for a variety of reasons, but in particular because

> the most calamitous effect of the new law and procedures will fall on research and training. Research in psychiatry depends upon enough hospital population to provide statistical validity with matched subjects, controlled in a variety of ways, over *a fully adequate time of close follow-up*. The new system will not allow this. Patients will also not be around long enough for adequate examination and treatment, and certainly not for adequate research study.[9]

The writer goes on to say that for the testing of new drugs and treatment measures many individuals are needed for long periods of observation, and that an in-and-out policy will eliminate much of this research work. These complaints about the lack of appropriate subjects for research were said to apply equally to the training of doctors in psychiatry, who need to see patients from a very large admission group over a long enough period of time to verify diagnosis and justify treatment choice. These editorials are important in that they so clearly reflect the belief that research and training needs take priority over the needs of the patient and over any concern for his civil liberties. The unspoken message is that the people we put in our mental hospitals do not count for much and what happens to them is of limited consequence.

There are additional reasons offered for continuing to hospitalize involuntarily. Some people are motivated by simple economics. The California State Employees Association, for example, some of whose members have jobs that depend upon certain levels of commitment, has lobbied for a return to easier civil commitments.[10] No doubt, others are motivated by ethical, professional, or religious feelings of responsibility to help. But it should be remembered that the history of the treatment of mental disorder is that people with excellent intentions have created dehumanizing situations.

The one thing that can be said with assurance is that in light of the many forces which come together in supporting continued use of involuntary hospitalization, reform will not be easily accomplished.

The Arguments for Involuntary Hospitalization

The discussion above regarding obstacles to change in a sense presents the arguments in favor of involuntary hospitalization. A restatement of the reasons offered for retaining involuntary hospitalization is appropriate here, a recent journal article was written expressly to make that case.[10] The following points offered in support of involuntary hospitalization are taken primarily but not exclusively from this article. The major benefits are said to be as follows:

1. The mentally ill can be identified and effectively treated.
2. At least some homicides, assaults, and suicides are prevented by involuntary hospitalization.
3. There are certain individuals—e.g., retardates, senile persons, regressed schizophrenics—who are unable to function in the community and need special care.
4. The rights of the individual are not paramount; the rights of the family and community must be recognized also.

5. Legal services which might not otherwise be available can be offered to a hospitalized patient.
6. Even if the status of a patient doesn't change, hospitalization allows time for the mobilization of resources for care in the community.
7. Patients rarely object to being on a locked ward. [11]
8. Hospitalization prevents behavior which is destructive of security and dignity.

Most of these points involve questionable assumptions. In many instances there is limited agreement as to who is mentally ill, and the effectiveness of treatment has not been demonstrated. Certainly some physical violence can be prevented by hospitalization, but it is probable that institutionalization facilitates some suicides. Helpless individuals are likely to enter the hospital voluntarily and a court order hardly seems necessary. With one exception the other objectives noted above are of lesser importance or could be achieved without coercion.

That exception relates to item no. 4, regarding the rights of the individual versus those of the family or community. It may be that we want to use compulsory hospitalization in the interest of maintaining social order and satisfying the desires of the community. But if we do, we should be overt about it, and we ought to carefully spell out the implications that such a decision would necessarily have. This point can be best illustrated by reference to an article which appeared in the *American Journal of Psychiatry* in 1975.[12] The authors—a psychiatrist, a psychologist, and a social worker—writing in support of involuntary hospitalization, cite the following incidents from their experience:

To directly relate our experiences to the main theme of this report, let us look into the reactions to closed ward treatment. It may be stated unequivocally that the community was strongly in favor of such a treatment modality and, at times, distressingly so. Not once in the two years of our study was there a complaint from any relative, group, or other interested party that we were locking up someone needlessly. Rather, the reverse was true. The pressure was clearly in the direction of treating more patients in the closed ward setting, and there were frequent requests from various individuals outside the hospital that patients be admitted to our ward.

We were confronted with the painful fact that the community does not understand, sympathize with, or want these individuals in its midst. Witness the following: In one case, persons representing themselves as spokesmen for an ethnically oriented social and political action group accompanied a patient to the admitting room of the hospital to assure her admission to a locked ward; they contended that she had thrown her newborn infant into a trash can on the street. Because of the nature of her behavior, and the social pressure, the patient was accepted for direct admission to the ICU. We later learned that the story was pure fabrication. The community had defined the patient as a nuisance, and it wanted to make sure that she stayed in the hospital.

In another instance, a young male patient arrived with several notes scrawled on the admitting papers sent from the community general hospital indicating that he was "to be admitted to a closed ward by order of Commissioner X [a name was given], New York City Department of Health." While we were under no obligation to heed these instructions, we did so. Within a day it was learned that no such commissioner existed. These examples illustrate the fact that community groups will go to great lengths, including subterfuge and misrepresentation, to rid themselves of the "troublesome" mentally ill.

Note that the above incidents are presented as part of an argument in support of involuntary hospitalization; yet, they serve rather to illustrate the problems connected with involuntary hospitalization, for apparently both of the individuals described were admitted to a closed ward without question. The authors go on to say that family desires are eminently clear in wanting patients to be kept in the hospital even when the staff feels that they are ready for discharge to the community. Given the incidents described in this hospital, an obvious implication is that the prospective patient should be afforded all of the protections of due process. In addition, it should be made clear to everyone that the hospital staff is concerned primarily with institutional and community interests as opposed to those of the individual. This kind of openness would force us to examine our purposes and possibly introduce a sense of fair play.

The evidence in favor of involuntary hospitalization is weak and indicates that if it should not be abolished altogether it certainly should be a rare event. When it does occur, it should be under the conditions that have been discussed in this book. We turn now to a summary of current trends and proposals for reform.

SOME PROPOSALS FOR REFORM

In spite of the resistance described above, we have noted elsewhere the generally high level of concern and activity surrounding commitment laws. These laws are an issue in each session of most state legislatures, and the trend is for the package of commitment laws to grow by the pound.

Law professor Ralph Slovenko is right in suggesting that criminal and tax laws appear simple by comparison, and that for the most part commitment laws are ignored because they are unnecessary or beyond the understanding of persons working in the field.[13] Dissatisfaction has continued to grow and has produced a number of conflicting recommendations for reform. The law journals, and to a lesser extent the social science and mental health journals, regularly contain recommendations for reform of one kind or another, with new impetus being provided by recent court decisions on the right to treatment.

By this point the reader should not be surprised to learn that the calls for reform do not all point in the same direction. At one extreme is the camp exemplified by Thomas Szasz, who would abolish all civil commitment laws. At the other extreme are those who would eliminate most civil commitment laws but turn the entire process over to the mental hospitals and departments of mental health, thereby removing it from legal safeguards.[14] Some favoring this latter position would be willing to beef up review procedures and safeguards that would come into play after hospitalization had taken place.

Somewhat short of turning things over completely to the hospitals is the suggestion of establishing a quasi-judicial commission of experts.[15] Proponents of this course argue that the commitment process calls for expertise but that the judgment should not take place within a courtroom atmosphere, where all the rules of law are brought into play. Administrative alternatives from other social problem areas are pointed to for precedent—e.g., workmen's compensation and juvenile courts. Safeguards would derive from the composition of the commission, which would consist of the various mental health professionals, an attorney, and possibly a layman. The presumed advantage of such a procedure would lie in the opportunity to mediate between legal and medical values while avoiding formal judicial procedures, which are thought to be harmful. The disadvantages lie in the assumptions that the proposal rests on. As we have seen, there is no reason to believe that the presence of an attorney guarantees the protection of legal rights or that the representation of several disciplines would ensure consideration of competing perspectives. Instead, it is highly probable that each commission would develop informal norms according to the particular biases and leadership contained within it. More importantly, the procedure assumes a base of knowledge and expertise from which to make decisions that does not exist.

Other proposals for changes in commitment laws are less sweeping and generally call for elaborations of existing statutes. The most frequent criticism of existing laws, and the one which is of greatest concern to lawyers, is in respect to the vagueness of terms employed in defining the criteria for involuntary hospitalization. The argument is that if we would just be specific in detailing what we mean by mental illness, dangerousness, etc., then the courts would have no problem in deciding when a person should be deprived of his freedom. The plea is made for the laws to spell out quantitatively the "degree of mental illness," or to require a judgment that the person is "more likely than not to commit a specific act within a specific time period."[16] Formulas are suggested that would take into account the number of errors that would be made in predicting future dangerousness of a particular kind and the relative seriousness of the dangerous behavior. The problem with all of this, of course, is that it assumes the ability to make such predictions or to quantify a definition of mental illness.

There is a certain surface validity and reasonableness inherent in some of the other proposals for change. For example, the law could reasonably require that there could be no commitment if a given illness is judged to be not treatable or if there is an expectation that treatment would not be provided because of inadequate personnel or facilities. If the reason for commitment is treatment but treatment is not possible, then clearly commitment is inappropriate. The difficulty with this suggestion is that it again assumes some consensus about what is treatable and what constitutes treatment.

Suggestions that the laws be revised to require exploration of alternatives to commitment—e.g., cases should be dismissed if the court feels that the individual is likely to be cooperative and could benefit from a program of voluntary treatment; guardians could be assigned—also seem reasonable on the surface. The problem is that these alternatives exist under current laws, and there is no reason to believe that spelling them out in detail would increase their use.

A relatively novel approach to reform grew out of a committee review of Wisconsin's mental health statutes.[17] The committee suggested that persons labeled "criminal" and persons labeled "mentally ill" should undergo the same kind of judicial decision-making process. That is, a decision to deprive persons of their rights would be based not on a condition called "mental illness" but on perceived danger or actual disruptive conduct. After the court had taken custody of a person, disposition would cover a definite term of confinement and would be made only after taking into consideration the available alternatives. The problem with this approach is that it is dependent upon expert testimony, and as the authors point out, the knowledge to make accurate predictions of behavior does not exist.

The Author's Proposals

It is unlikely that the abolition of civil commitment will occur in the immediate future. When abolition does happen, it is probable that it will result from a series of successive simplifications of current laws. The suggestions which follow are offered within this realistic perspective. The guiding principle is that civil commitment should be a rare event, and that the state does not have the right to control a person's body or behavior except under very compelling circumstances.

The only grounds for involuntary hospitalization should be that of physical dangerousness, and even this provision should be interpreted in a very narrow sense. Commitment proceedings should be legal in nature, based upon an adversary model, and governed by due-process procedures as outlined in this book. Very little beyond this is necessary.

Provisions for voluntary admission as they now exist in most state statutes should be abolished. Aside from the small number committed as dangerous, people would enter mental hospitals just as they do general medical hospitals, free to leave without notice or restraint.

There would be no provisions for "psychiatric emergencies," since these could be covered by current laws which deal with medical emergencies and crimes—e.g., passive, stuporous, noncommunicative persons would be treated legally like the unconscious; an aggressive person threatening violence would be treated like a person charged with a criminal offense.

A patient "Bill of Rights" does not have to be part of the statutes. Lengthy provisions regarding humane treatment, the right to free communication and privacy, transportation to the hospital, etc., imply that the mental patient loses a number of rights and thus it is necessary to spell out those he retains. Most of these rights are already guaranteed by law, and the only problem is to ensure that they are not abridged. For a good while to come it may be necessary to reaffirm various rights through documents internal to the hospital, but they need not be part of the mental health statutes.

Because of the continued thrust toward expanding the right-to-treatment doctrine,[18] there probably is a need in the short run for a provision that the patient have the right to refuse treatment even though involuntarily committed. There would also need to be some simple provisions for review after admission. Since the number of involuntary cases would be quite small, the review function should be relatively infrequent and not demanding of the staff's time.

Finally, the laws relating to involuntary commitment should provide for an authority outside of the Department of Mental Health to see that the law is enforced. The rights which have been won have limited meaning unless they are implemented, and this is never an easy task. The difficulty in enforcing rights has been well illustrated in the Miranda v. Arizona decision, which detailed the rights of criminal suspects. Recent studies suggest that the impact of this decision has been limited, and that much the same thing is now occurring with respect to court decisions on the rights of mental patients.[19] The enforcement authority would need to be well funded and staffed, particularly during the early phases of statutory reform being proposed here. If it did its job well, commitments would decrease rapidly and the staff size necessary to ensure compliance with the law could decrease proportionately.

There will be strong disagreement with the recommendations made here. The greatest concern will be that the criterion of dangerousness is too narrow—that society's desire for order and conformity should also be included. Case histories will be cited. Concern will be expressed about the person who wanders the streets, eats from garbage cans, and lives a degrading life. Someone will remember the eccentric who gives his money away on the streets or walks about with thousands of dollars sewn inside the lining of his coat. Others will object to sick people being held in jails instead of hospitals. Possibly the strongest outcry will be against those provisions which call for full due process and adversary proceedings within the courtroom.

In the larger context, these objections have little merit. However much we might wish it otherwise, our ability to predict dangerous behavior is extremely limited. The concept of social dangerousness is vague and subject to abuse, and allowing the state to restrain eccentrics of one kind or another could lead to severe infringements of rights which we value highly. It is obvious that there are instances in which state intervention may have prevented harm to helpless people. But the abuses under the current system of involuntary hospitalization far outweigh the advantages. Because of the limited expertise available in the field of mental illness, the major way to counter abuses is through invoking informal norms of behavior by employing laymen as decision makers.

What is being proposed represents a relatively radical departure, and bringing about the change will not be easy. Most departments of mental health, state mental health associations, and related groups will fight to retain current practices. There will have to be intensive educational programs for state legislatures, particularly with respect to the role of institutional psychiatry. Continued pressure through the courts will be necessary. Alternative services will have to be developed, particularly for the aged. But it is not an impossible task, and its ramifications could be truly far-reaching.

Implications of the Suggested Changes

In spite of arguments that change is hard to come by, some interesting things have happened in our state hospitals within the last few years. The number of patients has decreased, in some instances as much as 50 percent. The average length of stay for new admissions is now relatively short, often from three to six weeks. The patient population has changed, with relatively fewer old people and a marked increase in the number of persons with alcohol problems. In truth, the hospitals are less isolated and more open to public view than they have been, and the changes in the commitment laws being recommended here would accelerate the movement towards the hospital being a place of true asylum.

Those opposed to the growing interest in the civil liberties of mental patients frequently confuse this movement with a drive to eliminate mental hospitals and a belief in the minds of the civil libertarians that there are no people in need of hospitalization. Indeed, some of those in this movement probably have hopes of eliminating state mental hospitals rather than improving them. But it seems clear that there are a number of broken, socially incompetent people who need care and support. The recommendations made here do not deny that fact, but they would alter the conditions under which such care is given.

The elimination of coercion or the semblance of coercion

would affect all patient–staff interactions. Over time the staff might come to see itself as helpers rather than keepers, and in keeping with the nature of self-fulfilling prophecies the residents might assume more responsibility for their behavior and enter more cooperatively into treatment. Respect for constitutional rights would lead to a more humane atmosphere, and less stigma would be attached to having been a patient in a mental hospital.

The freeing of staff time to be devoted to supportive and therapeutic functions could be significant. Time devoted to the paperwork associated with compulsory hospitalization and to "discharge staffing" would be eliminated. The savings in time would affect the courts, freeing them to deal with the administration of justice, and the local sheriff would not have to detail two men to make the drive to the state hospital in order to deliver a patient. Legislative committees would not have to spend thousands of hours in the annual ritual of revising the commitment laws.

Proper enforcement of the suggested laws would encourage the development of alternative services. We could no longer go through the charade of having our old people declared mentally ill and warehoused under the guise of treatment. Rather than the currently developing practice of dumping some of these people back in the community without appropriate planning or care, we might be led to develop residential centers without all the overlay of a diagnosis of mental illness.

In those rare instances in which civil commitment was considered to be necessary, an open hearing under the rule of law could be quite functional. Open debate, media coverage, and adversary proceedings could bring into focus what it is that society will not tolerate at a given time. Instead of bemoaning the time taken by the courts in these relatively infrequent proceedings, we could see this as the court's contribution to the social order—the provision of a forum for establishing facts, and in the process making overt our reasons for segregating certain individuals. That is, the process could make us a more honest people in terms of the way we deal with troubled and troublesome people.

The recommendations being made in this book could provide a basis for a critical evaluation of the current roles of mental health professionals. We have referred elsewhere to the concern being expressed over the mental health professions serving as conservers of the status quo and as agents of social control. American analogues to the Russian practice of hospitalizing political dissenters are few in number, with Ezra Pound and General Edwin Walker being the two most frequently noted. But it has been recognized that in the wider sense of "political" the mental health professions may be said to perform a political function and mental health professionals may be caught up in a conflict between their institutional and instrumental roles. This holds particularly for those working in mental hospitals, prisons, schools, the armed forces, and other institutions.

There has been a tendency to redefine much of human experience in medical and psychiatric terms and to oversell on what can be delivered. Notions of omnipotence may have evolved from the prestige and financial rewards conferred upon the mental health professional. It is possible that study and open debate might lead us to be a bit more humble and a bit more sensitive to the social and moral judgments that are made within the context of a technical competence which is nonexistent or less extensive than we might wish. The need for a continuing critical analysis of the role of the mental health professional grows stronger with the increased talk about cooperation between the mental health and criminal justice system.

CONCLUDING OBSERVATIONS

Although this book has dealt only with civil commitment of people judged to be mentally ill, the basic problems described apply with equal force to those labeled as mentally retarded, disordered offenders, sexual offenders, alcoholics, and drug abusers. The fact that we have set up distinct institutions and provided distinct statutes for segregating those that offend does not mean that there is much rationality or reliability in our sorting behavior. There is marked overlap in the groupings and assignment to one category or another is highly problematic, having more to do with personal characteristics and administrative convenience than with behavior or scientific classification. Problems of definition, prediction, and control cut across each of the categories.

The failure of our mental hospitals and of institutions for the retarded, alcoholics, sexual offenders, etc., has been so widely recognized that further documentation here is unnecessary. Across these institutions, treatment has been minimal or nonexistent; the application of a disease model has been inappropriate; we have not been open about the coercive aspects of institutionalization and "treatment"; individual rights have been abridged; and we have not been sensitive to the political aspects of institutionalization and the role conflicts of professional staff in the institutions. Overriding all of this has been our confusion regarding our intentions. For the most part we have talked about the need to institutionalize in order to provide treatment and rehabilitation within a benevolent context. But this intention has been mixed with the desire to institutionalize as a means of punishment, or to simply isolate the person from the community.

We noted earlier the history of periodic demands for reform. It may be that for the first time events have come together in a way that allows us to move beyond questions of reform and to ask the more basic question of whether residential institutions, as we have known them, are really necessary. The decarceration movement, limited as it is, has roots which just might survive. It may be that we have finally recognized that there is nothing more destructive of a psychological sense of community than the act of segregation.[20]

In the short run, the greatest likelihood of bringing about change lies in the full utilization of legal processes. The suggestions made in that regard with respect to civil commitment apply equally to the related social problems noted above.

I hold no romantic notions that all residential institutions can be eliminated. Certainly there are people who must be segregated permanently or for long periods of time. I do hold that we are currently segregating many people unnecessarily and that society will be better off if we stop; and that those residential institutions that are necessary can be more humane and qualitatively different from those which we have known.

Notes and References

CHAPTER 1

1. D. L. ROSENHAN, "On Being Sane in Insane Places," *Science*, 1973, *179*, pp. 250–58.
2. "Most of St. Elizabeth's Patients Called Well Enough To Leave," *Washington Post*, August 11, 1971; W. Mendel and S. Rappeport, "Determinants of the Decision for Psychiatric Hospitalization," *Archives of General Psychiatry*, 1969, *20*, pp. 321–28.
3. F. D. CHU and S. TROTTER, *The Madness Establishment*, pp. 30–34.
4. A. DEUTSCH, *The Mentally Ill in America;* M. Foucault, *Madness and Civilization: A History of Insanity in the Age of Reason;* G. Rosen, *Madness in Society: Chapters in the Historical Sociology of Mental Illness*.
5. D. J. ROTHMAN, *The Discovery of the Asylum: Social Order and Disorder in the New Republic*.
6. FOUCAULT, p. 45.

7. Ibid., pp. 251–52.

8. Ibid., p. 268.

9. ROTHMAN, pp. 147–48.

10. FOUCAULT, p. 270.

11. See Rothman for a detailed history of the period up to 1920.

12. CHU and TROTTER, p. 34.

13. E. POLLACK and C. TAUBE, "Trends and Projections in State Hospital Use," paper presented at the symposium *The Future Role of the State Hospital,* Division of Community Psychiatry, State University of New York at Buffalo, Buffalo, N.Y., October 11, 1974, p. 14.

14. S. J. BRAKEL and R. S. ROCK, *The Mentally Disabled and the Law,* p. 17.

15. *American Psychological Association Monitor,* 1974, 5, no. 3, p. 1.

16. R. S. ROCK, M. A. JACOBSON, and R. M. JANOPAUL, *Hospitalization and Discharge of the Mentally Ill,* pp. 77–78.

17. Massachusetts General Laws, chapter 123, section 1 (1965). To its credit, the legislature finally rejected this concept of "social harm" in 1971.

18. *Psychiatric News,* July 18, 1973, p. 19.

19. *Psychiatric News,* November 7, 1973, p. 3.

20. See the series of articles appearing in the *Albany Times Union* between May 6 and May 11, 1975.

21. REICH and SIEGEL, "The Chronically Mentally Ill: Shuffle to Oblivion," *Psychiatric Annuals,* November, 1973. Additional references may be found in the *Harvard Law Review,* 1974, 87, pp. 1403–4.

22. National Institute of Mental Health, Federal Security

Agency, *A Draft Act Governing Hospitalization of the Mentally Ill*, Public Health Service Publication No. 51, 1952.

23. BRAKEL and ROCK.

24. Note: "Civil Commitment of the Mentally Ill," *Harvard Law Review*, 1974, *87*, pp. 1201–40.

25. J. A. GILBOY and J. R. SCHMIDT, "Voluntary Hospitalization of the Mentally Ill," *Northwestern University Law Review*, 1971, *66*, pp. 429–53.

26. J. W. ELLIS, "Volunteering Children: Parental Commitment of Minors to Mental Institutions," *California Law Review*, 1974, *62*, pp. 840–916.

27. B. M. BRAGINSKY, D. D. BRAGINSKY, and K. RING. *Methods of Madness: The Mental Hospital as a Last Resort*, pp. 49–74.

CHAPTER 2

1. DONALDSON v. O'CONNOR, *493* F., 2d *507*.

2. O'CONNOR v. DONALDSON, no. 74–8.

3. See S. A. SHAH, "Some Interactions of Law and Mental Health in the Handling of Social Deviance," *Catholic University of America Law Review*, 1974, *23*, 712–17, for a discussion of judicial default and possible remedies.

CHAPTER 3

1. T. J. SCHEFF, *Being Mentally Ill;* T. J. Scheff, "The Labelling Theory of Mental Illness," *American Sociological Review*, 1974, *39*, pp. 444–52; W. Gove, "Who Is Hospitalized: A Critical Review of Some Sociological Studies of Mental Illness," *Journal of*

Health and Social Behavior, 1970, *11*, pp. 294–303; W. R. Gove and P. Howell, "Individual Resources and Mental Hospitalization: A Comparison and Evaluation of the Societal Reaction and Psychiatric Perspectives," *American Sociological Review*, 1974, *39*, pp. 86–100; W. R. Gove, "Societal Reaction as an Explanation of Mental Illness: An Evaluation," *American Sociological Review*, 1970, *35*, pp. 873–84; Comments by Scheff, Gove, and Chauncey, *American Sociological Review*, 1975, *40*, pp. 242–57; A. W. Imershein and R. L. Simmons, "Rules and Examples in Lay and Professional Psychiatry: An Ethnomethodological Comment on the Scheff–Gove Controversy," *American Sociological Review*, 1976 (in press).

2. R. J. PLUNKETT and J. E. GORDON, *Epidemiology in Mental Illness;* B. Dohrenwend and B. S. Dohrenwend, "The Problem of Validity in Field Studies of Psychological Disorders," *Journal of Abnormal Psychology*, 1965, *70*, pp. 52–69.

3. L. SROLE et al., *Mental Health in the Metropolis: The Midtown Manhattan Study*, p. 138.

4. SCHEFF, *Being Mentally Ill*, p. 49.

5. B. J. ENNIS and T. R. LITWACK, "Psychiatry and the Presumption of Expertise: Flipping Coins in the Courtroom," *California Law Review*, 1974, *62*, pp. 694–752.

6. C. K. KANNO, *Eleven Indices*, Joint Information Service of the American Psychiatric Association and the National Association for Mental Health, 1971, p. 11.

7. M. A. BIRNBAUM, "Some Comments on 'The Right to Treatment,' " *Archives of General Psychiatry*, 1965, *13*, pp. 34–35.

8. D. OBERHAUSEN, H. M. KAPLAN, and K. S. MILLER, unpublished manuscript.

9. C. A. HANEY and R. MICHIELUTTE, "Selective Factors Operating in the Adjudication of Incompetency," *Journal of Health and Social Behavior*, 1968, *3*, pp. 233–42.

10. Ibid.

11. J. V. LOWRY and A. M. CALAIS, "Voluntary Community Treatment Can Prevent Admissions," *Hospital and Community Psychiatry*, 1967, *18*, pp. 236–37.

12. W. A. RUSHING, "Individual Resources, Societal Reaction, and Hospital Commitment," *American Journal of Sociology*, 1971, *77*, pp. 511–26; A. S. Linsky, "Who Shall Be Excluded: The Influence of Personal Attributes in Community Reaction to the Mentally Ill," *Social Psychiatry*, 1970, *5*, pp. 166–71; Gove and Howell, pp. 86–100.

13. HANEY and MICHIELUTTE, p. 239.

14. C. A. HANEY and S. B. FEIN, "Correlates of Social Distance and Gradients of Deviance," *Research Reports in Social Science*, Florida State University, 1968, *11*, pp. 25–41; J. J. See, "Ethnicity and Mental Incompetency Proceedings," unpublished Ph.D. dissertation, Florida State University, 1970.

15. J. J. See, p. 98.

16. C. A. HANEY, K. S. MILLER, and R. MICHIELUTTE, "The Interaction of Petitioner and Deviant Social Characteristics in the Adjudication of Incompetency," *Sociometry*, 1969, *32*, pp. 182–93.

17. Ibid.

18. C. A. HANEY and K. S. MILLER, "Definitional Factors in Mental Incompetency," *Sociology and Social Research*, 1970, *54*, pp. 520–31.

19. J. J. See, pp. 187–88.

20. HANEY and MICHIELUTTE, pp. 238–39.

21. S. B. FEIN and K. S. MILLER, "Legal Processes and Adjudication in Mental Incompetency Proceedings," *Social Problems*, 1972, *20*, pp. 57–64.

22. Ibid.

23. W. MENDEL and S. RAPPORT, "Determinants of the Decision for Psychiatric Hospitalization," *Archives of General Psychiatry*, 1969, *20*, pp. 321–28.

24. HANEY and MILLER, pp. 528–29.

25. J. J. See, pp. 167–72.

26. FEIN and MILLER, pp. 59–60.

CHAPTER 4

1. W. E. BRATTAIN, JR., et al., "The Charge of Mental Illness: A Study of the Rights and Statuses of the Mentally Ill in Florida," School of Social Welfare, Florida State University, 1970.

2. J. BRENNAN, "Mentally Ill Aggressiveness—Popular Myth or Reality?" *American Journal of Psychiatry*, 1964, *120*, pp. 1181–84.

3. United States v. Charnizon, 232 A. 2d *586, 588* (D. C. Cir. 1967).

4. MILLARD v. CAMERON, 373 F. 2d *468, 471* (1966); Cross v. Harris, 406 F. 2d *964, 978* (1968).

5. H. BRILL and B. MALZBERG, *Criminal Acts of Ex-Mental Hospital Patients,* American Psychiatric Association, Mental Hospital Service, Supplementary Mailing no. 153: 1962.

6. BRENNAN, pp. 1181–84.

7. J. Monahan, "The Prevention of Violence," in J. Monahan, ed., *Community Mental Health and the Criminal Justice System,* p. 19.

8. J. R. RAPPEPORT and G. LASSEN, "Dangerousness— Arrest Rate Comparisons of Discharged Patients and the General Population," *American Journal of Psychiatry,* 1965, *121,* pp. 776–83.

9. J. GIOVANNONI and L. GUREL, "Socially Disruptive Behavior of Ex–Mental Patients," *Archives of General Psychiatry,* 1967, *17,* pp. 146–53.

10. J. M. MULLEN and R. L. ROLLINS, *Factors of Assaultive Behavior in Mental Patients,* NIMH Grant Report 1R01 MH25263-01, April, 1975.

11. D. W. HASTINGS, "Follow-up Results in Psychiatric Illness," *American Journal of Psychiatry,* 1962, *118,* pp. 1078–86.

12. California State Legislature, Assembly Interim Committee on Ways and Means, Subcommittee on Mental Health Services, *The Dilemma of Mental Commitments in California,* 1967.

13. T. J. SCHEFF, *Being Mentally Ill,* pp. 131–32.

14. D. A. ALBERS, "Involuntary Hospitalization: Observations on the Politics of a Coalition," *South Dakota Law Review,* 1973, *18,* pp. 348–57.

15. J. MILLER, "Dangerous Behavior in First Admissions to a State Mental Hospital," unpublished Master's thesis, Florida State University, 1972.

16. Council of the American Psychiatric Association, "Position Statement on the Question of Adequacy of Treatment," *American Journal of Psychiatry,* 1967, *123,* pp. 1458–59.

17. U.S., Congress, Senate, Committee on the Judiciary, Subcommittee on Constitutional Rights, *Hearings on Constitutional Rights of the Mentally Ill*, 87th Cong., 1st sess., 1961, pt. *1*, 43.

18. J. M. MACDONALD, "Homicidal Threats," *American Journal of Psychiatry*, 1967, *124*, pp. 475–82.

19. M. A. BIRNBAUM, "A Rationale for the Right," in D. S. Burris, ed., *The Right to Treatment*, pp. 77–106.

20. B. J. ENNIS and T. R. LITWACK, "Psychiatry and the Presumption of Expertise: Flipping Coins in the Courtroom," *California Law Review*, 1974, *62*, pp. 693–752; J. Monahan, "Social Policy Implications of the Inability to Predict Violence," *Journal of Social Issues* (in press); J. J. Cocozz et al., "Some Refinements in the measurement and prediction of dangerous behavior," *American Journal of Psychiatry*, 1974, *131*, 1012ff; J. Monahan, "The Prediction of Violence," in D. Chappell and J. Monahan, eds., *Violence and Criminal Justice;* and J. Monahan, "Improving Predictions of Violence," *American Journal of Psychiatry* (in press). A. Dershowitz has elaborated extensively on the legal implications of the difficulties in predicting violence in "The Psychiatrists' Power in Civil Commitment," *Psychology Today*, 1969, *43, 2;* "Preventive Confinement: A Suggested Framework for Constitutional Analysis, *Texas Law Review*, 1973, *51, 1213;* and "The Law of Dangerousness: Some Fictions about Predictions," *Journal of Legal Education*, 1970, *23, 24*.

21. E. I. MEGARGEE, "The Prediction of Violence with Psychological Tests," in C. D. Spielberger, *Current Topics in Clinical and Community Psychology*, vol. 2.

22. J. MONAHAN, "Improving Predictions of Violence," *American Journal of Psychiatry* (in press).
23. D. MECHANIC, *Mental Health and Social Policy*, p. 122.
24. D. L. BAZELON, "The Law and the Mentally Ill," *American Journal of Psychiatry*, 1968, *125*, pp. 665–69.
25. E. S. SHNEIDMAN and N. L. FARBEROW, *Clues to Suicide*, p. 6–7.
26. N. D. RETTERSTÖL, *Long-Term Prognosis after Attempted Suicide*, Norwegian Research Council for Science and the Humanities, 1970.
27. A. D. POKORNY, "Characteristics of Forty-Four Patients who subsequently Committed Suicide." *Archives of General Psychiatry*, 1960, *2*, pp. 314–23.
28. SHNEIDMAN and FARBEROW, p. 9.
29. California State Legislature.
30. A comprehensive review has been provided by D. F. Greenberg in "Involuntary Psychiatry Commitments to Prevent Suicide." *New York University Law Review*, 1974, *49*, pp. 227–69.
31. S. L. HALLECK, *The Politics of Therapy*, p. 202; L. Jan, "Social Control Aspects of Hospitalization for Mental Illness," unpublished Ph.D. dissertation, Florida State University, 1974.

CHAPTER 5

1. M. FOUCAULT, *Madness and Civilization: A History of Insanity in the Age of Reason*, pp. 241–55.
2. K. JONES, *Mental Health and Social Policy, 1845–1959*, p. 126.
3. Ibid., p. 9.

4. R. BARTON and I. HAIDER, Unnecessary compulsory admissions to a psychiatric hospital, *Medicine, Science, and the Law*, 1966, *6*, pp. 147–50.

5. K. JONES, pp. 115–118.

6. Ibid., p. 126.

7. C. GREENLAND, "Appealing against Commitment to Mental Hospitals in the United Kingdom, Canada, and the United States: An International Review," *American Journal of Psychiatry*, 1969, *126*, pp. 538–42; H. P. Laughlin, "Psychiatry in the United Kingdom," *American Journal of Psychiatry*, 1970, *126*, pp. 1790–94; A. L. McGarry, "Law Medicine Notes: From Coercion to Consent," *New England Journal of Medicine*, 1966, *274*, p. 39.

8. D. BENNETT, "Community Mental Health Services in Britain," *The American Journal of Psychiatry*, 1973, *130*, pp. 1065–69.

9. *Report of the Royal Commission on the Law Relating to Mental Illness and Mental Deficiency, 1954–57*, May, 1957.

10. W. E. BARTON et al., *Impressions of European Psychiatry*, American Psychiatric Association, 1961, p. 23.

11. J. C. BARKER, Psychological Medical Group Conference, *British Medical Journal*, 1967, *3*, p. 245; R. Barton, "Misuse of Section 29, *Lancet*, 1966, *2*, pp. 1417–18; H. F. Patterson and A. R. Dobbs, "Section 29," *British Journal of Psychiatry*, 1963, *109*, pp. 202–5; J. A. Whitehead, "Misuse of Section 29," *Lancet*, 1965, *1*, p. 865; V. F. Jones, "Compulsory Observation Admissions to Hospitals and Units for the Mentally Ill in the Liverpool Region," Department of Health and So-

cial Security, Liverpool Region, 1969, Mimeographed Document 69/310.

12. M. D. ENOCH and J. C. BARKER, "Misuse of Section 29: Fact or Fiction?" *Lancet,* 1965, *1,* pp. 760–61.

13. M. MARKOWE, Letter to the editor, *British Medical Journal,* 1967, *2,* p. 703.

14. V. F. JONES.

15. ENOCH and BARKER.

16. BARTON and HAIDER. pp. 147–50.

17. BARTON.

18. ENOCH and BARKER; PATTERSON and DOBBS; G. MILNER, "Compulsory Observation Admissions to a Comprehensive Psychiatric Unit," *Medical Officer,* 1966, *115,* p. 293; R. Barton and I. Haider, "Misuse of Section 29," *Lancet,* 1965, *1,* p. 912.

19. M. D. EILENBERG, M. J. PRITCHARD, and P. B. WHATMORE, A Twelve Month Survey of Observation Ward Practice," *British Journal of Preventive and Social Medicine,* 1962, *16,* pp. 22–29.

20. A. R. C. LAWSON, *The Recognition of Mental Illness in London,* Institute of Psychiatry, Maudsley Monographs #5, Oxford Press, 1966.

21. PATTERSON and DOBBS.

22. K. S. MILLER, R. L. SIMONS and S. B. FEIN, "Compulsory Mental Hospitalization in England and Wales," *Journal of Health and Social Behavior,* 1974, *15,* pp. 151–56.

23. LAWSON.

24. H. DAWSON, "Reasons for Compulsory Admission," in J. K. Wing and A. M. Hailey, eds., *Evaluating a Community Psychiatric Service.*

25. D. G. MORGAN and R. M. COMPTON, "Psychiatric In-patients and Out-patients: A Reply to Mezey and Evans," *British Journal of Psychiatry*, 1972, *120*, pp. 433–36.

26. W. E. BARTON, M. J. FARRELL, F. T. LENEHAN, and W. F. McLAUGHLIN, *Impressions of European Psychiatry*, American Psychiatric Association, 1961, p. 24.

27. GREENLAND. A broader analysis may be found in C. Greenland, *Mental Illness and Civil Liberty*, Occasional Papers on Social Administration #38, G. Bell and Sons, 1970.

28. "Note re Applications to Review Tribunals, *British Medical Journal*, 1969, *1*, p. 522.

29. Quoted in the St. Petersburg, Florida, *Times*, May 17, 1971. See also Department of Health and Social Security: Committee of Inquiry into Conditions at Whittingham Hospital, Command 4861, London, Her Majesty's Stationery Office, 1972.

30. *Lancet*, 1973, *2*, pp. 165–66.

31. "Patients' Rights: The Mentally Disordered in Hospital," Mind Report No. 10, National Association for Mental Health, 39 Queen Anne Street, London WIM OAJ.

32. Mental Patients' Union Newsletter, 97 Prince of Wales Road, London N.W. 5.

33. BENNETT, p. 1067.

34. F. J. J. LETEMENDIA and A. D. HARRIS, "Psychiatric Services and the Future," *Lancet*, 1973, *2*, pp. 1013–16.

CHAPTER 6

1. Group for the Advancement of Psychiatry, *Laws Governing Hospitalization of the Mentally Ill,* 1966, Report No. 61.

2. American Bar Association, Special Committee on the Rights of the Mentally Ill, *Reports of the American Bar Association,* 1947, *72,* p. 289.

3. See Y. KUMASAKA and R. K. GUPTA, "Lawyers and Psychiatrists in the Court: Issues on Civil Commitment," *Maryland Law Review,* 1972, xxxii, pp. 6–35, for an analysis of conceptual, definitional, and attitudinal differences between lawyers and psychiatrists in civil commitment proceedings. S. W. Baernstein, "Functional Relations between Law and Psychiatry: A Study of Characteristics Inherent in Professional Interaction," *Journal of Legal Education,* 1971, *23,* pp. 399–423, describes contrasting emphases upon external and internal factors.

4. R. B. REA, "The Rights of the Mentally Ill: A Proposal for Procedural Changes in Hospital Admission and Discharge," *Psychiatry,* 1966, *29,* pp. 213–26, contrasts the Illinois Mental Health Code (primarily legal in orientation) with the (primarily medical) New York Code.

5. See C. W. COMBS, "Burden of Proof and Vagueness in Civil Commitment Proceedings," *American Journal of Criminal Law,* 1973, *2,* pp. 47–66, for a detailed discussion of statutory specificity and proof beyond a reasonable doubt.

6. H. A. DAVIDSON, *Forensic Psychiatry.* A recent sur-

vey by L. Steinmork and S. Nagel suggests that United States psychiatrists are not as opposed to due process in commitment proceedings as the earlier literature had indicated. Their findings apply to all aspects of due process, but as the authors indicate, a response rate of 38 percent might reflect a biased sample. "The Impact of Due Process Rules on Commitment Proceedings," mimeographed paper available from the authors, University of Illinois.

7. A. BRODERICK, "Justice in the Books or Justice in Action: An Institutional Approach to Involuntary Hospitalization for Mental Illness," *Catholic University Law Review,* 1971, *20,* p. 676.

8. S. J. BRAKEL and R. S. ROCK, *The Mentally Disabled and the Law,* p. 51.

9. Quoted by R. T. ROTH in "Emergency Commitment Laws: A Due Process Emergency," *The Abolitionist,* 1973, *3,* p. 3.

10. MULLANE v. Cent. Hanover Bank and Trust Co., 339 U.S. 306, 314 (1950).

11. See Note: "Compulsory Commitment: The Rights of the Incarcerated Mentally Ill," *Duke Law Journal,* 1969, p. 691, for court decisions relating to requirement of notice.

12. LESSARD v. SCHMIDT, 349 F. Supp. 1078, 1092 (E.D. Wis. 1972).

13. K. S. MILLER, A. M. HARTSFIELD, and D. OBERHAUSEN, "Changes in State Laws for Involuntary Civil Commitment, 1959–69, *Governmental Research Bulletin,* Florida State University, 1971, *8,* no. 2.

14. S. B. FEIN and K. S. MILLER, "Legal Processes and

Adjudication in Mental Incompetency Proceedings,'' *Social Problems*, 1972, *20*, pp. 57–64.

15. L. L. LANGDALE, ''Civil Commitment of the Mentally Ill in Nebraska,'' *Nebraska Law Review*, 1968, *48*, p. 263.

16. BRAKEL and ROCK, p. 52.

17. D. J. KOCHER, ''Involuntary Commitment Procedures in Missouri,'' *University of Missouri, Kansas City, Law Review*, 1969, *37*, p. 328.

18. Note: ''Mental Illness and Due Process: Involuntary Commitment in New York,'' *New York Law Forum*, 1970, *16*, p. 165.

19. T. R. LITWACK, ''The Role of Counsel in Civil Commitment Proceedings: Emerging Problems,'' *California Law Review*, 1974, *62*, 821–23.

20. F. COHEN, ''The Function of the Attorney and the Commitment of the Mentally Ill,'' *Texas Law Review*, 1966, *44*, p. 425; R. Maisel, ''Decision-making in a Commitment Court,'' *Psychiatry*, 1970, *33*, pp. 352–61; D. Miller and M. Schwartz, ''County Lunacy Commission Hearings: Some Observations of Commitments to a State Mental Hospital,'' *Social Problems*, 1966, *14*, pp. 25–26; R. S. Rock, M. A. Jacobson and R. M. Janopaul, *Hospitalization and Discharge of the Mentally Ill;* T. J. Scheff, ''Social Conditions for Rationality: How Urban and Rural Courts Deal with the Mentally Ill,'' *The American Behavioral Scientist,* March, 1964, pp. 21–24; T. J. Scheff, ''The Societal Reaction to Deviance: Ascriptive Elements in the Psychiatric Screening of Mental Patients in a Midwestern State,'' *Social Problems*, 1964, *11*, pp. 401–13; California State Legislature, Subcommittee on Mental Health Services,

The Dilemma of Mental Commitments in California, 1967; W. A. Wilde, "Decision-making in a Psychiatric Screening Agency," *Journal of Health and Social Behavior,* 1968, *9,* pp. 215–21; Fein and Miller; L. Kutner, "The Illusion of Due Process in Commitment Proceedings," *Northwestern Law Review,* 1962, *57,* pp. 383–99; G. E. Dix, "Acute Psychiatric Hospitalization of the Mentally Ill in the Metropolis: An Empirical Study," *Washington University Law Quarterly,* 1968, *4,* pp. 485–591.

21. KOCHER, pp. 329–30.

22. Y. KUMASAKA, "The Lawyer's Role in Involuntary Commitment—New York's Experience," *Mental Hygiene,* 1972, *56,* p. 24.

23. Note: "Civil Commitment of the Mentally Ill," *Harvard Law Review,* 1974, *87,* p. 1281.

24. M. P. RABINOWITZ, "Constitutional Law—Civil Commitment Proceedings—Due Process Required," *Mississippi Law Journal,* 1973, *44,* p. 547.

25. BRAKEL and ROCK, p. 54–55.

26. ROCK, JACOBSON, and JANOPAUL, p. 184.

27. D. L. WENGER and C. R. FLETCHER, "The Effect of Legal Counsel on Admissions to a State Mental Hospital: A Confrontation of Professions," *Journal of Health and Social Behavior,* 1969, *10,* pp. 66–72; Fein and Miller; Cohen, p. 441; L. V. Kaplan, "Civil Commitment 'as you like it,' " *Boston University Law Review,* 1969, *49,* p. 36; R. Bolton, "Legislative Initiative in the Mental Health Field," *State Government,* 1968, *41,* pp. 187–193.

28. KAPLAN, p. 36; T. R. Litwack, "The Role of Counsel in Civil Commitment Proceedings: Emerging Problems," *California Law Review,* 1974, *62,* 816–39.

29. See KOCHER, pp. 350–51, for observations of proceedings in a Missouri court. He reports the absence of witnesses, formal defense, and cross-examination. See also N. Beran and S. Dinitz, "An Empirical Study of the Psychiatric Probation–commitment Procedure," *American Journal of Orthopsychiatry,* 1973, *43,* 660–69.

30. COHEN, p. 441.

31. Ibid., p. 428.

32. BRAKEL and ROCK, p. 158.

33. M. BLINICK, "Mental Illness and the Lawyer's Professional Responsibility," *The Practical Lawyer,* 1970, *16,* p. 39.

34. KUMASAKA and GUPTA, p. 32.

35. WENGER and FLETCHER, p. 69.

36. KAPLAN, p. 37.

37. California State Legislature, p. 41.

38. LESSARD V. SCHMIDT, 349 F. Supp. 1078, 1100–02 (E.D. Wis. 1972), vacated and remanded on other grounds, 94 S. Ct. 713 (1974). See also Note: *Harvard Law Review,* 1974, *87,* 1303–13, for a detailed discussion of the privilege against self-incrimination.

39. SHAH, 712–13.

40. FEIN and MILLER, p. 59.

41. WENGER and FLETCHER, p. 68.

42. J. J. SEE, "Ethnicity and Mental Incompetency Proceedings," unpublished Ph.D. dissertation, Florida State University, 1970.

43. D. MECHANIC, *Mental Health and Social Policy*, pp. 126–127.

44. FEIN and MILLER, pp. 60–61.

45. R. E. PFRENDER, "Probate Court Attitudes Toward Involuntary Hospitalization: A Field Study," *Journal of Family Law*, 1965, *5*, pp. 139–57.

46. M. BIRNBAUM, "Right to Treatment," *American Bar Association Journal*, 1960, *46*, p. 499; M. Birnbaum, "Some Comments on 'The Right to Treatment,' " *Archives of General Psychiatry*, 1965, *13*, pp. 34–45; M. Birnbaum, "A Rationale for the Right," in D. S. Burris, ed., *The Right to Treatment*, pp. 77–106.

47. L. B. KASSINER, "The Right to Treatment and the Right to Refuse Treatment—Recent Case Law," *Journal of Psychiatry and the Law*, 1974, *2*, 456–70; J. Robitscher, "Courts, State Hospitals, and the Right to Treatment," *American Journal of Psychiatry*, 1972, *129*, 298–304.

48. ROUSE v. CAMERON, 373 F. 2d 451 (D.C. Cir. 1966).

49. WYATT v. STICKNEY, 344 F. Supp. 373 and 344 F. Supp. 387 (M.D. Alabama, 1972).

50. American Psychological Association Monitor, *6*, September–October, 1975, p. 8.

51. BURNHAM v. Department of Public Health, 349 F. Supp. 1335 (N.D. Ga. 1972).

52. TRIBBY v. CAMERON, 379 F. 2d 104 (D.C. Cir. 1967); Williams v. Robinson, 432 F. 2d 637 (D.C. Cir. 1970); United States v. Ecker, 479 F. 2d 1206, 1210 (D.C. Cir. 1973).

53. WYATT v. ADERHOLT, 43 U.S. L.W. 2208 (5th Cir., Nov. 8, 1974).

54. See the discussion by Kassiner, pp. 462–65; and J. W. Ellis, "Volunteering Children: Parental Commitment of Minors to Mental Institutions," *California Law Review*, 1974, *62*, p. 858, footnote no. 106.

55. LAKE V. CAMERON, 364 F. 2d 657 (D.C. Cir. 1966); Lessard v. Schmidt, 349 F. Supp. 1078 (E.D. Wis. 1972).

56. S. A. SHAH, "Some Interactions of Law and Mental Health in the Handling of Social Deviance," *Catholic University of America Law Review*, 1974, *23*, 693–97.

57. See Note: *Harvard Law Review*, 1974, *87*, 1207–21, for a detailed discussion.

58. LESSARD V. SCHMIDT.

59. In re Ballay, 482 F. 2d 648 (D.C. Cir. 1973).

60. References no. 5 and 56 above.

61. R. SLOVENKO, "Civil Commitment in perspective," *Journal of Public Law*, 1971, *20*, pp. 3–32.

62. W. J. CURRAN, "Community Mental Health and the Commitment Laws: A Radical New Approach Is Needed," *American Journal of Public Health*, 1967, *57*, pp. 1565–70.

63. BRAKEL and ROCK, p. 60.

64. JACKSON V. INDIANA, 406 U.S. 715 (1972).

65. D. L. CHAMBERS, "Alternatives to Civil Commitment of the Mentally Ill: Practical Guides and Constitutional Imperatives," *Michigan Law Review*, 1972, *70*, p. 1110.

CHAPTER 7

1. W. E. BARTON, *Administration in Psychiatry*, chapter V, p. 1.

2. J. H. JACKSON, K. S. MILLER, and H. M. KAPLAN, "The Florida Mental Health Act: An Assessment of Impact," *Governmental Research Bulletin*, Florida State University, 1973, *10*, no. 2.

3. R. SLOVENKO, "Civil Commitment in Perspective," *Journal of Public Law*, 1971, *20*, pp. 3–32.

4. JUDY MILLER, "APA: Psychiatrists Reluctant to Analyze Themselves," *Science*, July, 1973, pp. 246–48.

5. *American Psychological Association Monitor*, April, 1974, *5*, no. 4, p. 1.

6. Personal communication from the American Psychological Association.

7. L. BELLAK, "The Need for Public Health Laws for Psychiatric Illness," *American Journal of Public Health*, 1971, *61*, pp. 119–21.

8. S. RACHLIN, A. PAM, and J. MILTON, "Civil Liberties Versus Involuntary Hospitalization," *American Journal of Psychiatry*, 1975, *132*, p. 191.

9. Editorial comment: "Law's Labor Lost," *Psychiatric Quarterly*, 1966, *40*, p. 156. See also Editorial comment: "Mental Hygiene Law—1967," *Psychiatric Quarterly*, 1967, *41*, pp. 766, 768–69.

10. R. PEELE, P. CHODOFF, and N. TAUB, "Involuntary Hospitalization and Treatability: Observations from the District of Columbia Experience," *Catholic University of America Law Review*, 1974, *23*, 744–53.

11. RACHLIN et al. (see reference no. 8 above) quote Fischer and Weinstein, *Archives of General Psychiatry*, 1971, *25*, pp. 41–48, as saying that in the readmission of former patients there was not one instance in ten years in which the locked door was objected to by either the

patient or his relatives. Rachlin et al. say that their experience was the same.

12. See reference no. 8 above.

13. R. SLOVENKO.

14. W. J. CURRAN, "Community Mental Health and the Commitment Laws: A Radical New Approach is Needed," *American Journal of Public Health,* 1967, *57,* pp. 1565–70.

15. R. B. REA, "The Rights of the Mentally Ill: A Proposal for Procedural Changes in Hospital Admission and Discharge," *Psychiatry,* 1966, *29,* 213–26.

16. R. I. POSTEL, "Civil Commitment: A Functional Analysis," *Brooklyn Law Review,* 1971, *38,* pp. 1–94.

17. N. E. PENN et al., "Some Considerations for Future Mental Health Legislation," *Mental Hygiene,* 1969, *53,* pp. 10–13.

18. In September, 1975, Morton Birnbaum filed a right-to-treatment suit in New York in the hope of resolving a number of the questions that the Supreme Court left unanswered in Donaldson. *New York Times,* September 25, 1975.

19. A. MEISEL, "Rights of the Mentally Ill: The Gulf between Theory and Reality," *Hospital and Community Psychiatry,* 1975, *26,* pp. 349–53.

20. For a detailed development of this theme, see S. B. Sarason, *The Psychological Sense of Community.*

Bibliography

ALBERS, D. A. "Involuntary hospitalization: Observations on the Politics of a Coalition." *South Dakota Law Review*, 1973, *18*, 348–57.

American Psychological Association Monitor, 1974, *5*, no. 3, p. 1.

American Psychological Association Monitor, 1974, *5*, no. 4, p. 1.

BAERNSTEIN, S. W. "Functional Relations between Law and Psychiatry: A Study of Characteristics Inherent in Professional Interaction." *Journal of Legal Education*, 1971, *23*, 399–423.

BARKER, J. C. "Psychological Medical Group Conference," *British Medical Journal*, 1967, *3*, 245.

BARTON, R. "Misuse of Section 29." *Lancet*, 1966, *2*, 1417–18.

BARTON, R. and HAIDER, I. "Misuse of Section 29." *Lancet*, 1965, *1*, 912.

BARTON, R., and HAIDER, I. "Unnecessary Compulsory Admissions to a Psychiatric Hospital." *Medicine, Science, and the Law*, 1966, *6*, 147–50.

164

BARTON, W. E. *Administration in Psychiatry*. Charles C. Thomas, 1962.

BARTON, W. E., FARRELL, M. J., LENEHAN, F. T., and McLAUGHLIN, W. F. *Impressions of European Psychiatry*. American Psychiatric Association, 1961.

BAZELON, D. L. "The Law and the Mentally Ill." *American Journal of Psychiatry*, 1968, *125*, 665–69.

BELLAK, L. "The Need for Public Health Laws for Psychiatric Illness." *American Journal of Public Health*, 1971, *61*, 119–21.

BENNETT, D. "Community Mental Health Services in Britain." *American Journal of Psychiatry*, 1973, *130*, 1065–69.

BERAN, N., and DENITZ, S. "An Empirical Study of the Psychiatric Probation–Commitment Procedure." *American Journal of Orthopsychiatry*, 1973, *43*, 600–69.

BIRNBAUM, M. "Right to Treatment." *American Bar Association Journal*, 1960, *46*, 499.

BIRNBAUM, M. "Some Comments on 'The Right to Treatment.'" *Archives of General Psychiatry*, 1965, *13*, 34–45.

BIRNBAUM, M. A. "A Rationale for the Right," in D. S. Burris, ed., *The Right to Treatment*. Springer Publishing Co., 1969.

BLINICK, M. "Mental Illness and the Lawyer's Professional Responsibility." *The Practical Lawyer*, 1970, *16*, 37–43.

BOLTON, R. "Legislative Initiative in the Mental Health Field." *State Government*, 1968, *41*, 187–93.

BRAGINSKY, B. M., BRAGINSKY, D. D., and RING, K. *Methods of Madness: The Mental Hospital as a Last Resort*. Holt, Rinehart and Winston, 1969.

BRAKEL, S. J., and ROCK, R. S. *The Mentally Disabled and the Law* (rev. ed.) University of Chicago Press, 1971.

BRATTAIN, W. E., JR.; GRIFFIN, M. D.; PROCTOR, J.; PROCTOR, R. H., RILEY, D. E., ROBERTS, K., and SMITH, S. "The Charge of Mental Illness: A Study of the Rights and Statuses of the Mentally Ill in Florida." School of Social Welfare, Florida State University, 1970.

BRENNAN, J. "Mentally Ill Aggressiveness—Popular Myth or Reality?" *American Journal of Psychiatry,* 1964, *120,* 1181–84.

BRENNER, M. H. *Mental Illness and the Economy.* Harvard University Press, 1973.

BRILL, H., and MALZBERG, B. *Criminal Acts of Ex-Mental Hospital Patients.* American Psychiatric Association, Mental Hospital Service, Supplementary Mailing No. 153:1962.

BRODERICK, A. "Justice in the Books or Justice in Action—An Institutional Approach to Involuntary Hospitalization for Mental Illness." *Catholic University of America Law Review,* 1971, *20,* 547–701.

California State Legislature, Subcommittee on Mental Health Services. *The Dilemma of Mental Commitments in California,* 1967.

CHAMBERS, D. L. "Alternatives to Civil Commitment of the Mentally Ill: Practical Guides and Constitutional Imperatives." *Michicagn Law Review,* 1972, *70,* 1108–1200.

CHAUNCEY, R. L. "Comment on Scheff." *American Sociological Review,* 1975, *40,* 248–52.

CHU, F. D., and TROTTER, S. *The Madness Establishment:* Ralph Nader's Study Group Report on the National Institute of Mental Health. Grossman Publishers, 1974.

COCOZZ, J. J., and STEADMAN, H. J. "Some Refinements in the Measurement and Prediction of Dangerous Behavior." *American Journal of Psychiatry*, 1974, *131*, 1012–14.

COHEN, F. "The Function of the Attorney and the Commitment of the Mentally Ill." *Texas Law Review*, 1966, *44*, 424–67.

COMBS, C. W. "Burden of Proof and Vagueness in Civil Commitment Proceedings," *American Journal of Criminal Law*, 1973, *2*, 47–66.

Council of the American Psychiatric Association, "Position Statement on the Question of Adequacy of Treatment." *American Journal of Psychiatry*, 1967, *123*, 1458–59.

CURRAN, W. J. "Community Mental Health and the Commitment Laws: A Radical New Approach is Needed." *American Journal of Public Health*, 1967, *57*, 1565–70.

DAVIDSON, H. A. *Forensic Psychiatry*. Ronald Press, 1965.

DAWSON, H. "Reasons for Compulsory Admission," in J. K. Wing and A. M. Hailey, eds., *Evaluating a Community Psychiatric Service*. Oxford University Press, 1972.

DERSHOWITZ, A. M. "The Psychiatrist's Power in Civil Commitment: A Knife That Cuts Both Ways." *Psychology Today*, 1969, *43*, 42–47.

DERSHOWITZ, A. M. "The Law of Dangerousness: Some Fictions about Predictions." *Journal of Legal Education*, 1970, *23*, 24.

DERSHOWITZ, A. M. "Preventive Confinement: A Suggested Framework for Constitutional Analysis." *Texas Law Review*, 1973, *51*, 1213.

DEUTSCH, A. *The Mentally Ill in America* (rev. ed.). Doubleday & Company, 1949.

DIX, G. E. "Acute Psychiatric Hospitalization of the Mentally Ill in the Metropolis: An Empirical Study." *Washington University Law Quarterly,* 1968, *4,* 485–591.

DOHRENWEND, BRUCE, and DOHRENWEND, B. S. "The Problem of Validity in Field Studies of Psychological Disorder." *Journal of Abnormal Psychology,* 1965, *70,* 52–69.

Editorial comment: "Law's labor lost." *Psychiatric Quarterly,* 1966, *40,* 150, 156–57.

Editorial comment: "Mental Hygiene Law—1967." *Psychiatric Quarterly,* 1967, *41,* 766, 768–769.

EILENBERG, M. D., PRITCHARD, M. J., and WHATMORE, P. B. "A twelve-month Survey of Observation Ward Practice." *British Journal of Preventive and Social Medicine,* 1962, *16,* 22–29.

ELLIS, J. W. "Volunteering Children: Parental Commitment of Minors to Mental Institutions." *California Law Review,* 1974, *62,* 840–916.

ENNIS, B. J., and LITWACK, T. R. "Psychiatry and the Presumption of Expertise: Flipping Coins in the Courtroom." *California Law Review,* 1974, *62,* 693–752.

ENOCH, M. D., and BARKER, J. C. "Misuse of Section 29—Fact or Fiction?" *Lancet,* 1965, *1,* 760–61.

FEIN, S. B., and MILLER, K. S. "Legal Processes and Adjudication in Mental Incompetency Proceedings." *Social Problems,* 1972, *20,* 57–64.

FOUCAULT, M. *Madness and Civilization: A History of Insanity in the Age of Reason* (trans. R. Howard), Pantheon Books, 1965.

GILBOY, J. A., and SCHMIDT, J. R. "Voluntary Hospitalization of the Mentally Ill." *Northwestern University Law Review,* 1971, *66,* 429–53.

GIOVANNONI, J., and GUREL, L. "Socially Disruptive Behavior of Ex–Mental Patients." *Archives of General Psychiatry*, 1967, *17*, 146–53.

GOVE, W. R. "Who is Hospitalized: A Critical Review of Some Sociological Studies of Mental Illness." *Journal of Health and Social Behavior*, 1970, *11*, 294–303.

GOVE, W. R. "Comment on Scheff." *American Sociological Review*, 1975, *40*, 242–48.

GOVE, W. R., and HOWELL, P. "Individual Resources and Mental Hospitalization: A Comparison and Evaluation of the Societal Reaction and Psychiatric Perspectives." *American Sociological Review*, 1974, *39*, 86–100.

GREENBERG, D. F. "Involuntary Psychiatric Commitments to Prevent Suicide: Social Science and Social Policy." *New York University Law Review*, 1974, *49*, 227–69.

GREENLAND, C. "Appealing against Commitment to Mental Hospitals in the United Kingdom, Canada, and the United States: An International Review." *American Journal of Psychiatry*, 1969, *126*, 538–42.

GREENLAND, C. *Mental Illness and Civil Liberty:* Occasional Papers on Social Administration #38. G. Bell & Sons, 1970.

Group for the Advancement of Psychiatry. *Laws Governing Hospitalization of the Mentally Ill*. 1966, Report No. 61.

HALLECK, S. L. *The Politics of Therapy*. Science House, 1971.

HANEY, C. A., and FEIN, S. B. "Correlates of Social Distance and Gradients of Deviance." *Research Reports in Social Science*, Florida State University, 1968, *11*, 25–41.

HANEY, C. A., and MICHIELUTTE, R. "Selective Factors

Operating in the Adjudication of Incompetency." *Journal of Health and Social Behavior,* 1968, *3,* 233–42.

HANEY, C. A., and MILLER, K. S. "Definitional Factors in Mental Incompetency." *Sociology and Social Research,* 1970, *54,* 520–31.

HANEY, C. A., MILLER, K. S., and MICHIELUTTE, R. "The Interaction of Petitioner and Deviant Social Characteristics in the Adjudication of Incompetency." *Sociometry,* 1969, *32,* 182–93.

HASTINGS, D. W. "Follow-up Results in Psychiatric Illness." *American Journal of Psychiatry,* 1962, *118,* 1078–86.

IMERSHEIN, A. W., and SIMONS, R. L. "Rules and Examples in Lay and Professional Psychiatry: An Enthomethodological Comment on the Scheff–Gove Controversy." *American Sociological Review,* 1976 (in press).

JACKSON, J. H., MILLER, K. S., and KAPLAN, H. M. "The Florida Mental Health Act: An Assessment of Impact." *Governmental Research Bulletin,* Florida State University, 1973, *10,* no. 2.

JAN, L. "Social Control Aspects of Hospitalization for Mental Illness." Unpublished Ph.D. dissertation, Florida State University, 1974.

JONES, K. *Mental Health and Social Policy, 1845–1959.* Routledge & Kegan Paul, 1960.

JONES, V. F. "Compulsory Observation Admissions to Hospitals and Units for the Mentally Ill in the Liverpool Region," Mimeographed Document 69/310. Department of Health and Social Security, Liverpool Region, 1969.

KANNO, C. K. *Eleven Indices.* Joint Information Service of

the American Psychiatric Association and the National Association for Mental Health, 1971.

KAPLAN, L. V. "Civil Commitment 'As You Like It.' " *Boston University Law Review*, 1969, *49*, 14–45.

KASSIVER, L. B. "The Right to Treatment and the Right to Refuse Treatment—Recent Case Law," *Journal of Psychiatry and Law*. 1974, *2*, 456–70.

KINDRED, M. *The Mentally Retarded Citizen and the Law*. The Free Press, 1976.

KITTRIE, N. N. *The Right to be Different*, Pelican, 1973.

KOCHER, D. J. "Involuntary Commitment Procedures in Missouri." *University of Missouri, Kansas City, Law Review*, 1969, *37*, 319–51.

KUMASAKA, Y. "The Lawyer's Role in Involuntary Commitment—New York's Experience." *Mental Hygiene*, 1972, *56*, 21–29.

KUMASAKA, Y., and GUPTA, R. K. "Lawyers and Psychiatrists in the Court: Issues on Civil Commitment." *Maryland Law Review*, 1972, xxxii, 6–35.

KUTNER, L. "The Illusion of Due Process in Commitment Proceedings." *Northwestern Law Review*, 1962, *57*, 383–99.

LANGDALE, L. L. "Civil Commitment of the Mentally Ill in Nebraska." *Nebraska Law Review*, 1968, *48*, 255–71.

LAUGHLIN, H. P. "Psychiatry in the United Kingdom." *American Journal of Psychiatry*, 1970, *126*, 1790–94.

LAWSON, A. R. C. *The Recognition of Mental Illness in London*. Institute of Psychiatry, Maudsley Monographs #5. Oxford Press, 1966.

LETEMENDIA, F. J. J., and HARRIS, A. D. "Psychiatric Services and the Future." *Lancet*, 1973, *2*, 1013–16.

LINSKY, A. S. "Who Shall Be Excluded: The Influence of Personal Attributes in Community Reaction to the Mentally Ill." *Social Psychiatry,* 1970, *5,* 166–71.

LITWACK, T. R. "The Role of Counsel in Civil Commitment Proceedings: Emerging Problems." *California Law Review,* 1974, *62,* 816–39.

LOWRY, J. V., and CALAIS, A. M. "Voluntary Community Treatment Can Prevent Admissions." *Hospital and Community Psychiatry,* 1967, *18,* 236–37.

MCGARRY, A. L. "Law Medicine Notes: From Coercion to Consent." *New England Journal of Medicine,* 1966, *274,* 39.

MCGARRY, A. L., and KAPLAN, H. A. "Overview: Current Trends in Mental Health Law." *The American Journal of Psychiatry.* 1973, *130,* 621–30.

MACDONALD, J. M. "Homicidal Threats." *American Journal of Psychiatry,* 1967, *124,* 475–82.

MAISEL, R. "Decision-making in a Commitment Court." *Psychiatry,* 1970, *33,* 352–61.

MARKOWE, M. "Letter to the Editor." *British Medical Journal,* 1967, *2,* 703.

Massachusetts General Laws. Ch. 123, Sect. 1 (1965).

MECHANIC, D. *Mental Health and Social Policy.* Prentice-Hall, 1969.

MEGARGEE, E. I. "The Prediction of Violence with Psychological Tests," in C. D. Spielberger, *Current Topics in Clinical and Community Psychology,* vol. 2. Academic Press, 1970.

MEISEL, A. "Rights of the Mentally Ill: The Gulf between Theory and Reality." *Hospital and Community Psychiatry,* 1975, *26,* 349–53.

MENDEL, W., and RAPPORT, S. "Determinants of the Decision for Psychiatric Hospitalization." *Archives of General Psychiatry,* 1969, *20,* 321–28.

Mental Health Law Project, *Basic Rights of the Mentally Handicapped.* Mental Health Law Project, 1751 N Street, N.W., Washington, D.C. 20036, 1973.

MILLER, D., and SCHWARTZ, M. "County Lunacy Commission Hearings: Some Observations of Commitments to a State Mental Hospital." *Social Problems,* 1966, *14,* 21–27.

MILLER, J. "Dangerous Behavior in First Admissions to a State Mental Hospital." Unpublished Master's thesis, Florida State University, 1972.

MILLER, J. APA: "Psychiatrists Reluctant to Analyze Themselves." *Science,* 1973, *179,* 246–48.

MILLER, K. S.; HARTSFIELD, A. M.; and OBERHAUSEN, D. "Changes in State Laws for Involuntary Civil Commitment, 1959–1969." *Governmental Research Bulletin,* Florida State University, 1971, *8,* no. 2.

MILLER, K. S., SIMONS, R. L., and FEIN, S. B. "Compulsory Mental Hospitalization in England and Wales." *Journal of Health and Social Behavior,* 1974, *151,* 151–56.

MILNER, G. "Compulsory Observation Admissions to a Comprehensive Psychiatric Unit." *Medical Officer,* 1966, *115,* 293.

MONAHAN, J. "The Prediction of Violence," in D. Chappell and J. Monahan, eds., *Violence and Criminal Justice.* Lexington Books, 1975.

MONAHAN, J. "The Prevention of Violence," in J. Monahan, ed., *Community Mental Health and the Criminal Justice System.* Pergamon Press, 1975.

MONAHAN, J. "Improving Predictions of Violence." *American Journal of Psychiatry* (in press).

MONAHAN, J. "Social Policy Implications of the Inability to Predict Violence." *Journal of Social Issues* (in press).

MORGAN, D. G., and COMPTON, R. M. "Psychiatric In-Patients and Out-Patients: A Reply to Mezey and Evans." *British Journal of Psychiatry,* 1972, *120,* 433–36.

"Most of St. Elizabeth's Patients Called Well Enough to Leave." *Washington Post,* August 11, 1971.

MULLEN, J. M., and ROLLINS, R. L. "Factors of Assaultive Behavior in Mental Patients." NIMH Grant Report 1R01 MH25263-01. April, 1975.

National Institute of Mental Health, Federal Security Agency. *A Draft Act Governing Hospitalization of the Mentally Ill.* Public Health Service Publication No. 51, 1952.

"Note: Civil Commitment of the Mentally Ill." *Harvard Law Review,* 1974, *87,* 1190–1406.

"Note: Compulsory Commitment: The Rights of the Incarcerated Mentally Ill." *Duke Law Journal,* 1969, 677–732.

"Note: Mental Illness and Due Process: Involuntary Commitment in New York." *New York Law Forum,* 1970, *16,* 165–86.

"Patients' Rights: The Mentally Disordered in Hospitals." Mind Report No. 10. National Association for Mental Health, 32 Queen Anne Street, London WIM OAJ.

PATTERSON, H. F., and DOBBS, A. R. "Section 29." *British Journal of Psychiatry,* 1963, *109,* 202–5.

PEELE, R., CHODOFF, P., and TAUB, N. "Involuntary Hospitalization and Treatability: Observations from the

District of Columbia Experience." *Catholic University of America Law Review,* 1974, *23,* 744–53.

PENN, N. E., STOVER, D., GIEBINK, J., and SINDBERG, R. "Some Considerations for Future Mental Health Legislation." *Mental Hygiene,* 1969, *53,* 10–13.

PFRENDER, R. E. "Probate Court Attitudes toward Involuntary Hospitalization: A Field Study." *Journal of Family Law,* 1965, *5,* 139–57.

PLUNKETT, R. J., and GORDON, J. E. *Epidemiology in Mental Illness.* Basic Books, 1960.

POKORNY, A. D. "Characteristics of Forty-Four Patients Who Subsequently Committed Suicide." *Archives of General Psychiatry,* 1960, *2,* 314–23.

POLLACK, E. S., and TAUBE, C. A. "Trends and Projections in State Hospital Use." Paper presented at the symposium on *The Future Role of the State Hospital,* Division of Community Psychiatry, State University of New York at Buffalo, Buffalo, N.Y., October 11, 1974.

POSTEL, R. I. "Civil Commitment: A Functional Analysis." *Brooklyn Law Review,* 1971, *38,* 1–94.

RABINOWITZ, M. P. "Constitutional Law—Civil Commitment Proceedings—Due Process Required." *Mississippi Law Journal,* 1973, *44,* 544–49.

RACHLIN, S., PAM, A., and MILTON, J. "Civil Liberties versus Involuntary Hospitalization." *American Journal of Psychiatry,* 1975, *132,* 189–91.

RAPPEPORT, J. R., and LASSEN, G. "Dangerousness: Arrest Rate Comparisons of Discharged Patients and the General Population." *American Journal of Psychiatry,* 1965, *121,* 776–83.

REA, R. B. "The Rights of the Mentally Ill: A Proposal for

Procedural Changes in Hospital Admission and Discharge." *Psychiatry*, 1966, *29*, 213–26.

Report on the Royal Commission on the Law Relating to Mental Illness and Mental Deficiency, 1954–1957. May, 1957.

RETTERSTÖL, N. D. *Long-term Prognosis after Attempted Suicide.* Norwegian Research Council for Science and the Humanities, 1970.

ROBITSCHER, J. D. "Courts, State Hospitals, and the Right to Treatment." *American Journal of Psychiatry*, 1972, *129*, 298–304.

ROCK, R. S., JACOBSON, M. A., and JANOPAUL, R. M. *Hospitalization and Discharge of the Mentally Ill.* University of Chicago Press, 1968.

ROSEN, G. *Madness in Society: Chapters in the Historical Sociology of Mental Illness.* University of Chicago Press, 1968.

ROSENHAN, D. L. "On Being Sane in Insane Places." *Science*, 1973, *179*, 250–58.

ROTH, R. T. "Emergency Commitment Laws: A Due Process Emergency." *The Abolitionist*, 1973, *3*, no. 1.

ROTHMAN, D. J. *The Discovery of the Asylum: Social Order and Disorder in the New Republic.* Little, Brown and Co., 1971.

RUSHING, W. A. "Individual Resources, Societal Reaction, and Hospital Commitment." *American Journal of Sociology*, 1971, *77*, 511–26.

SARASON, S. B. *The Psychological Sense of Community.* Jossey-Bass, 1974.

SCHEFF, T. J. "Social Conditions for Rationality: How

Urban and Rural Courts Deal with the Mentally Ill." *The American Behavioral Scientist,* March, 1964, 21–24.

SCHEFF, T. J. "The Societal Reaction to Deviance: Ascriptive Elements in the Psychiatric Screening of Mental Patients in a Midwestern State." *Social Problems,* 1964, *11,* 401–13.

SCHEFF, T. J. *Being Mentally Ill.* Aldine, 1966.

SCHEFF, T. J. "The Labelling Theory of Mental Illness." *American Sociological Review,* 1974, *39,* 444–52.

SCHEFF, T. J. "Reply to Chauncey and Gove." *American Sociological Review,* 1975, *40,* 252–57.

SEE, J. J. "Ethnicity and Mental Incompetency Proceedings." Unpublished Ph. D. dissertation, Florida State University, 1970.

SHAH, S. A. "Some Interactions of Law and Mental Health in the Handling of Social Deviance." *Catholic University of America Law Review,* 1974, *23,* 674–719.

SHNEIDMAN, E. S., and FARBEROW, N. L. *Clues to Suicide.* McGraw-Hill, 1957.

SLOVENKO, R. "Civil Commitment in Perspective." *Journal of Public Law,* 1971, *20,* 3–32.

SROLE, L., LANGNER, T. S., MICHAEL, S. T., OPLER, M. K. and RENNIE, T. A. C. *Mental Health in the Metropolis: The Midtown Manhattan Study.* McGraw-Hill, 1962.

STEINMARK, L., and NAGEL, S. "The Impact of Due Process Rules on Commitment Proceedings." Mimeographed paper available from the authors at the University of Illinois.

SZASZ, T. S. *Law, Liberty, and Psychiatry.* Macmillan, 1963.

WENGER, D. L., and FLETCHER, C. R. "The Effect of Legal Counsel on Admissions to a State Mental Hospital: A Confrontation of Professions." *Journal of Health and Social Behavior,* 1969, *10,* 66–72.

WHITEHEAD, J. A. "Misuse of Section 29." *Lancet,* 1965, *1,* 865.

WILDE, W. A. "Decision-making in a Psychiatric Screening Agency." *Journal of Health and Social Behavior,* 1968, *9,* 215–21.

U.S., Congress, Senate, Committee on the Judiciary, Subcommittee on Constitutional Rights. *Hearings on Constitutional Rights of the Mentally Ill.* 87th Cong., 1st sess., 1961, pt. 1, 43.

Index

Index

Albers, D. A., 164
American Bar Association, 13, 94
American Civil Liberties Union, 13, 22
American Psychiatric Association, 13, 14, 124

Baernstein, S. W., 155, 164
Barker, J. C., 81, 152, 153, 164, 168
Barton, R., 81–82, 152, 153, 164
Barton, W. E., 93, 152, 154, 161, 165
Baxstrom v. Herold, 60–61
Bazelon, D. L., 151, 165
Beers, C., 8
Bellak, L., 126, 162, 165, 167
Bennett, D., 152, 154, 165
Beran N., 159, 165
Birnbaum, M. A., 64–65, 113, 146, 150, 160, 163, 165
Blinick, M., 159, 165
Bolton, R., 158, 165
Bosch, H., 4
Braginsky, B. M., 145, 165
Braginsky, D. D., 145, 165
Brakel, S. J., 105, 144, 145, 156, 157, 158, 159, 161, 166
Brattain, W. E., 148, 166
Brennan, J., 60, 148, 166

Brenner, M. H., 166
Brill, H., 59, 148, 166
Broderick, A., 156, 166
Burnham v. Department of Public Health, 115
Burris, D. S., 150, 160, 165

Calais, A. M., 147, 172
Caminez, J., 29
Chambers, D. L., 161, 166
Chapell, D., 173
Chauncey, R. L., 166
Chodoff, P., 162, 174
Chu, F. D., 143, 144, 166
Cocozz, J. J., 150, 167
Coffer, H., 29
Cohen, F., 93, 104, 157, 159, 167
Combs, C. W., 117, 155, 167
Commitment laws, current assessment, 119–20
Compton, R. M., 154, 174
Compulsory hospitalization, variability, England, 84–87
Conolly, J., 76
Court and Examining Committee, 108–111
Curran, W., 119, 161, 163, 167

Dangerousness, among hospital patients, 59–65
Davidson, H. A., 155, 167
Dawson, H., 85, 153, 167
Deinstitutionalization, 15
Denitz, S., 159, 165
Dershowitz, A., 150, 167
Deutsch, A., 4, 143, 167
Dix, G. E., 158, 168
Dobbs, A. R., 152, 153, 174
Dohrenwend, B. P., 146, 168
Dohrenwend, B. S., 146, 168
Donaldson, K., 19–26, 113
Dostoevski, 1
Draft Act Governing Hospitalization of the Mentally Ill, 16

Eilenberg, M. D., 153, 168
Ellis, J. W., 145, 161, 168
Ennis, B. J., 146, 150, 168
Enoch, M. D., 81, 153, 168
Examining committee composition, 111–12

Fair, J., 19, 26–35
Farberow, N. L., 71, 151
Farrell, M. J., 154, 165
Fein, S. B., 43, 44, 51, 54, 83, 84, 109, 147, 148, 153, 156, 158, 159, 160, 168, 169, 173
Fletcher, C. R., 106, 109, 158, 159, 178
Foucault, M., 4, 6, 76, 143, 151, 168

Giebink, J., 175
Gilboy, J. A., 145, 168
Giovannoni, J., 62, 169
Goffman, I., 12
Gordon, J. E., 146, 175
Gove, W. R., 37, 145, 146, 147, 169
Greenberg, D. F., 151, 169
Greenland, C., 152, 154, 169
Griffin, M. D., 166
Group for the Advancement of Psychiatry, 94
Gumanis, J., 22

Gupta, R. K., 155, 159, 171
Gurel, L., 62, 169

Haider, I., 81, 152, 153, 164
Hailey, A. M., 153, 167
Halleck, S. L., 151, 169
Haney, C. A., 43, 44, 46, 50, 52, 147, 148, 169, 170
Hanwell Hospital, 76
Harris, A. D., 154, 171
Hartsfield, A. M., 156, 173
Hastings, D. W., 170
Hearing, 101–102
Hospitalization, 79–112
  conflict between law and medicine, 94–97
  England, background, 76–78
  major categories, 16
Hospitalization rates,
  variability, 39–42
    interstate, 40
    intrastate, 40–41
Howell, P., 146, 147, 169

Imershein, A. W., 170
Involuntary hospitalization, 8
  appeals against, England, 87–88
  arguments in favor, 128–31
  coercion, 86–87
  forces for reform, England, 88–91
  implications of suggested changes, 138–42
  involvement of attorneys, 103–106
  proposals for reform, 131–41
  recent court decisions, 112–18
  resistance to reform, 122–28
  significance, 8–11
  signs of unrest, 11–15
  standard of proof, 116–17

Jackson, J. H., 162, 175
Jacobson, M. A., 144, 157, 158, 176
Janopaul, R. M., 144, 157, 158, 176
Jan, L., 151, 170
Jean, P., 93
Jones, K., 151, 152, 170

Jones, V. F., 81, 152, 153, 170
Jury trial, 107, 108

Kanno, C. K., 146, 170
Kaplan, H. M., 146, 162, 170, 172
Kaplan, L. V., 158–59, 171
Kassiver, L. B., 160, 161, 171
Kindred, M., 171
Kittrie, N. N., 12, 171
Kocher, D. J., 157, 158, 159, 171
Kumasaka, Y., 155, 158, 159, 171
Kutner, L., 158, 171

Laing, R., 12
Langdale, L. L., 157, 171
Langner, T. S., 177
Lassen, G., 61, 175
Laughlin, H. P., 152, 171
Lawson, A. R. C., 85, 153, 171
Least restrictive alternative doctrine, 115
Leifer, R., 12
Lembcke, J., 21
Lenehan, F. T., 154, 165
Letemendia, F. J. J., 154, 171
Linsky, A. S., 172
Litwack, T. R., 146, 150, 157, 159, 168, 172
Lowry, J. V., 147, 172

MacDonald, J. M., 64, 150, 172
Maisel, R., 157, 172
Malzberg, B., 59, 148, 166
Mapperley Hospital, Nottingham, 77
Markowe, M., 153, 172
McGarry, A. L., 152, 172
McLaughlin, W. F., 154, 165
Mechanic, D., 63, 119, 151, 160, 172
Medical model, 36–37
Megargee, E. I., 66–67, 150, 172
Meisel, A., 163, 172
Mendel, W., 143, 148, 173
Mental Health Act of 1959, 78–88
    Section 29, 79–83
Mental health law project, 22

Mental hospital:
    admission rates, 3
    expenditures, 8
    treatment rates, 9
Mental hospitalization:
    behavior of alleged incompetent, 51–55
    detention status, 54–55
    examining committee composition, 49–50
    role of the court, 47–51
    role of others, 46–47
    role of personal characteristics, 42–46
    violence, 53–54
Mental incompetency, loss of civil rights, 9
Mental patient, historical treatment, 4–8
Merckle, A. M., 28
Michael, S., 177
Michielutte, R., 43, 46, 50, 147, 148, 169, 170
Mill, J. S., 57
Miller, D., 157, 173
Miller, Jan, 63, 173
Miller, Judy, 162
Miller, K. S., 46, 51, 52, 54, 83, 84, 109, 146, 147, 148, 153, 156, 158, 159, 160, 162, 168, 170, 173
Milner, G., 153, 173
Milton, J., 162, 175
Miranda v. Arizona, 136
Monahan, J., 60, 150, 151, 173, 174
Morgan, D. G., 154, 174
Mullen, J. M., 174

Nagel, S., 156, 177
National Association for the Abolition of Involuntary Mental Hospitalization, 13
New York mental hygiene law, 127
Notice, 98–101

Oberhausen, D., 146, 156, 173
O'Connor, J. B., 21

O'Connor v. Donaldson, implications and unresolved questions, 24–26
Ogburn, B., 29
Opler, T., 177

Pam, A., 162, 175
Parens patriae doctrine, 16, 116
Patterson, H. F., 152, 153, 174
Peele, R., 162, 174
Penn, N. E., 163, 175
Perender, R. E., 175
Pfrender, S., 112, 160
Pinel, 6
Plunkett, R. J., 146, 175
Pokorny, A. D., 70, 151, 175
Pollack, E. S., 144, 175
Postel, R. I., 163, 175
Pound, E., 140
President's Commission on Mental Retardation, 14
Pritchard, M. J., 153, 168
Proctor, J., 166
Proctor, R. H., 166
Psychiatric diagnosis, reliability and validity, 38–39
Psychiatric disorders, prevalence, 37–38

Rabinowitz, M. P., 158, 175
Rachlin, S., 162, 175
Rappeport, J. R., 175
Rapport, S., 143, 148, 173
Rea, R. B., 155, 163, 175
Reagan, Governor, 14
Rennie, T. A. C., 177
Retterstöl, N. D., 70, 151, 176
Right to refuse treatment, 115
Right to remain silent, 34, 108
Riley, D. E., 166
Ring, K., 145, 165
Roberts, K., 166
Robitscher, J. D., 160, 176
Rock, R. S., 105, 106, 144, 145, 156, 157, 158, 159, 161, 166, 176

Rollins, R. L., 174
Rosen, G., 4, 143, 176
Rosenhan, D. L., 143, 175, 176
Roth, R. T., 156, 176
Rothman, D. J., 4, 143, 144, 176
Rouse v. Cameron, 113–14
Royal Commission on Mental Illness and Mental Deficiency, 77, 83
Rushing, W. A., 147, 176

Sarason, S. B., 163
Scheff, T. J., 12, 37, 145, 146, 157, 176, 177
Schmidt, J. R., 145, 168
Schwartz, M., 157, 173
See, J. J., 43, 44, 45, 48, 53, 147, 148, 159, 177
Shah, S. A., 145, 159, 161, 177
Shneidman, E. S., 71, 151, 177
Simons, R. L., 83, 84, 146, 153, 170, 173
Sindberg, R., 175
Slovenko, R., 118, 132, 161, 162, 163, 177
Smith, S., 166
Societal reaction perspective, 36, 37
Society for Individual Freedom, 14, 89
Spielberger, C. D., 150, 172
Srole, L., 146, 177
Steadman, H. J., 167
Steinmark, L., 156, 177
Stover, D., 175
Suicide, 69–72
Supreme Court, 120
    Donaldson decision, 24
Szasz, T., 132, 177

Taub, N., 174
Taube, C. A., 144, 175
Thomas, A. C., 177
Trotter, S., 143, 144, 166
Tuke, 6

Violence, prediction, 65–69

Walker, General, E., 140
Wenger, D. L., 106, 109, 158, 159, 178
Whatmore, P. B., 153, 168
Whitehead, J. A., 152, 178

Wilde, W. A., 158, 178
Wing, J. K., 153, 167
Wyatt v. Aderholt, 114, 115
Wyatt v. Stickney, 114